**FOREWORD BY PHIL LENIR**
Co-Founder and President of CoachingOurselves

# THRIVING
## IN THE
# MIDDLE

Why Managers Need to
be Coaching Each Other

# MIKE COOK

*"There is no need to sally forth, for it remains true that those things which make us human are, curiously enough, always close at hand. Resolve, then, that on this very ground, with small flags waving and tiny blasts of tiny trumpets, we shall meet the enemy, and not only may he be ours, he may be us."*

—Walt Kelly, creator of Pogo

# DEDICATION

This is for all the management development professionals who have spent countless hours working to enhance the lives of their fellow employees by supporting the development of managers with empathy and a willingness to experience their own vulnerability. It is my hope that what is offered here will open new perspectives for you and move you toward the fulfillment of why you chose this profession.

# ACKNOWLEDGMENT

This book was made possible by the support and encouragement of my remarkable wife, Pat Jackson, who never gives me an inch to not give my absolute best and remains my most honest critic.

# TABLE OF CONTENTS

# FOREWORD

Modern organizations are strange places indeed. Many of us spend a large portion of our life working in organizations. We work together in teams and groups to create the products and deliver the services which form such a large part of our lives and our society. The modern form of our organizations has changed very little in comparison to the changes in technology and society. Most of us, quite unconsciously, still see organizations as the machine organizations of the early 20th century. Human resources are neatly laid out on an organizational chart with clear roles and responsibilities. Hierarchies and chains of accountability are the glue through which the organizational machine produces products or delivers services efficiently and effectively. Wages provide the motivation for the human resources, while profits drive the owners. This interplay ensures the whole system is optimized and aligned for individual, organizational, and societal needs.

It all sounds so neat and rational. But at some point, usually quite early in our career, many of us realize this is not how things work. It's a simplification largely derived from the thinking of economists. There aren't any human resources working in organizations, only human beings. Organizational charts, rigid roles and responsibilities, competency frameworks, and yearly performance reviews all tend to diminish organizational performance rather than help. Though people need good wages and generally like making money, there are many other, far more important motivational factors driving human beings to genuinely commit towards achieving common organizational goals. And there is a whole host of contextual factors, such as trust and collaboration, far more important to improving results than individual performance.

It was in mid-2014 when Mike Cook first reached out to Henry Mintzberg and I at CoachingOurselves. He has this lovely warm and affable manner which is quite charming, and I immediately warmed up to him. Unlike some experts in our industry, Mike has both a broad view and a practical focus. I've spent much of my career working as an engineer and have an aversion for anything impractical or academic.

In many ways, Mike reminds me of Ed Schein but with a strong focus on the middle managers who make up the bulk of our organizations. Mike's perspectives on organizations and organizational life, human motivations, and people development are rich and layered from his three decades of experience.

Mike and I spent the last three years working together. We focused primarily on how managers and leaders can develop in a way that results in improved organizational performance. In a machine-like view of organizations, it's easy to believe that if human resources were trained to perform according to the prescribed competencies, then overall organizational performance would increase. But of course, this never seems to happen.

However, over the past 15 years or so, a host of pragmatic approaches with strong results have taken root. The world of leadership and management development is now going through a ferocious series of changes similar to those engulfing many aspects of the traditional HR function.

Mike and I hoped to write a book together, but I frankly never had the focus Mike possesses. So Mike went ahead and wrote his own book, which you have in front of you now. As I read the manuscript I got quite excited. Many of the themes of our discussions were laid out and brought to life with Mike's well-crafted stories. I hope you enjoy this book, and I hope it will influence you and many others to change the way we develop ourselves, our teams, and our organizations for the benefit of society and everyone who comes after us.

Phil Lenir, Co-Founder and President,
CoachingOurselves
Visit: www.CoachingOurselves.com

# INTRODUCTION

"We need to work harder, not smarter!" We have heard this phrase so often in recent years that you may not have noticed the misquote. "We...need...to work...HARDER...not smarter." No offense intended, as they say.

This is not just a sassy way to start a book. The point here is that we've heard the phrase, "We need to work smarter, not harder" so many times and then gone right back to working harder. The axiom no longer has any power, and in most cases, we haven't noticed. But as the saying also goes, "Take heart, oh ye of little faith!" This book was written because I hope to help you truly work smarter—though it might not look like you expect.

I live in Anacortes, Washington, where the ferries leave for the San Juan Islands and Victoria, BC. The city is situated on Fidalgo Island, and since it isn't very large—40 square miles—it is fairly easy to find your way around. One geographic challenge for visitors, and even many of the locals, is to keep the names and locations of the island's eight fresh water lakes straight. One of them is Heart Lake, known to be a fine place to catch bass.

If you travel south from 41st Street on O Avenue, you'll find yourself heading to the outer rim of the island. Along the way you'll pass a hand-lettered sign nailed on a telephone pole. Here is what the sign says… "This is not the road to Heart Lake."

So now we know. O Avenue is not the way to Heart Lake. If we were looking for Heart Lake, this information would let us know it is time to stop heading this way. If we were not looking for Heart Lake, we can make note for the future.

What we obviously don't know at this point, however, is how to find our way to Heart Lake.

My wife and I now use the phrase, "This is not the way to Heart Lake" as shorthand for letting each other know that what one of us may have just communicated to the other does not contain sufficient information to be useful.

"This is not the way to Heart Lake" is how I feel about much of what goes on today in the management development within organizational life. If business is about results and return on investment, then the return on investment for the time and money spent on management education must be rigorously questioned. For most management development, the results are fuzzy at best. One thing we have learned with certainty is that not much of what goes on in traditional classroom-style management development ever makes its way back into the workplace as improved managing. In fact, much of it doesn't make it to the cars in the parking lot; experts tell us that about

50 percent of what is covered in a typical classroom-type development setting is forgotten within two weeks.[1] After the first two weeks, the drop-off rate is even more dramatic, eventually plunging towards a plateau of around 10 percent of remembered material, including where you put the learning manual and the instructor's name.

Can we at least agree on this? It's definitely not the road to Heart Lake. But…it just might fit the definition of insanity taken from Alcoholics Anonymous: "Doing the same thing over and over expecting a different outcome."

Realize that this does not paint a very promising picture for management development going forward. However, if we have been on the wrong road as pertains to this objective, maybe we'd do ourselves a favor by stopping what we've been doing, standing back, and observing the natural flow in the workplace for a while. Remember…that sign says THIS is not the road to Heart Lake, not that there is NO ROAD to Heart Lake! The implication is clear: There is a road, but this isn't it, so we need to keep looking.

Where do managers spend their time? What are they doing while they are there? Is it possible they may be learning in these settings too? And, if they are, how might we account for that and facilitate it?

This book is an assertion, with some evidence thrown in for support, that to find what we are really seeking, which is to know what we look like when we are truly working smarter, we will have to give up or at least set aside some long-held beliefs and fundamental views about development in general. More precisely, to shift our view of management development/education from being solely constituted of a periodic series of events to being one of continuous practice. Rather than an emergency fix or an event with a beginning, middle, and end, development is always occurring. How do we capture that?

Management development is an emergent phenomenon, only visible in the moment of action, never finished, and virtually unmeasurable. It's much more process than destination. Unmeasurable makes us very uncomfortable. In fact, unmeasurable makes us so uncomfortable that we would rather measure the wrong thing than go forward on faith having measured nothing at all.

If that notion makes you uncomfortable, this one will make you more so. The greatest untapped asset in any organization may be the embedded knowledge base of the management community. If you can accept this assertion on faith, you are on the road to Heart Lake.

This is a book for developing managers. It is not about how to manage. It is about a way to develop managers that corresponds to the way managing unfolds on a daily basis; more a tutorial for building a framework of development. There is no "done" with management development, there is no "over," no graduation, no final certification. There is today, and what we did or did not do, and what we can learn from it in either case. There is the love and challenge of managing, and setting yourself up to enjoy managing.

At its heart, managing is about people. It's about the time of their lives, making that time worthwhile, and making a buck at the same time; oh yes, and the contribution that you are driven to make. This book is about thriving in the middle of it all and being proud of it.

If you are an operational-level manager, what follows may sound like Nirvana. Your skepticism is healthy; you've been tricked countless times. If you are a senior manager, especially one responsible for talent development, this approach may turn your world on its head. You may feel horror at the money you've wasted. Don't worry, we can help you recover some of the cost and improve your ROI, but it will take patience and learning to live with the reality that you'll never be able to do more than offer correlation. There will be no cause and effect relationship if you follow the approach we recommend. If you are someone who has devoted your life to developing managers, my claims may seem threatening. Don't worry; you are the baby, not the bathwater. There is a place for you in this new world I'll be describing. It won't offer that traditional place at the front of the room or up on the platform, but it will offer the opportunity to make both a real difference in your organization and help create environments of natural engagement.

As much as anything, *Thriving in the Middle* is a challenge. The popular thing is to offer solutions, but when it comes to people and managing, there can be no guarantees; simply shared experience and the hint of a direction in which to travel.

# PART 1

## AN ENTIRELY NEW WAY TO THINK ABOUT MANAGEMENT DEVELOPMENT

"Wouldn't it be great if we could do our physical fitness all in one year then be done with it? The way we currently address management development makes about as much sense."

—Mike Cook

# CHAPTER 1
# WHY THIS BOOK?

Do we really need another book on managing? We can answer that question simply: No, there is no need at this time for any more books on how to manage. So this is not that kind of book. However, a radical reimagining of the role and value of operational-level managers is called for at this time.

It is our firmly held belief that operational-level managers are both a key element of operational success as well as the catalyst for any organization to work smarter. In order to develop these core contributors to operational success, a new appreciation of what it means to "manage in the middle" must be created and supported. Any such approach will orient thinking towards the customer first, hierarchy second. Managers will begin to see their world primarily flowing at them from the customer's desires rather than senior management's directives. The development of managers will reflect this reorientation and become much more like the work itself, rather than the heretofore methods of varying degrees of simulation. Such an approach will break the cycles of:

- Managers being *sent* to development programs rather than choosing to attend

- Increasingly unaffordable developmental programs requiring extensive travel costs and time away from work

- One-size-fits-all immersion style (week-long residential) training with limited relevance to specific manager challenges and offering little or no framework for applying course content on the job

- Solo study of online material offering no practical value, and lacking the added benefits of collective sharing of experience and learning

The description that follows represents a breakthrough in thinking and execution of the professional development of operational-level managers.

Through thousands of hours of action research embedded in real-life management environments, a set of observations has emerged that connect seemingly trivial or unrelated conditions:

- Most managers hold operational-level positions.

- Most of these individuals will remain operational-level throughout their careers for legitimate reasons, not for lack of opportunity or talent. Their talents are uniquely suited to this level of management.

- There are distinctly unique skills involved in being a strong performer at the operational-level of management over time.

- Managers who are driven to attain a senior-level position will leave an organization rather than accept long-term employment in the middle or front line.

- The primary value of operational-level managers is the development and retention of talent within an organization.

- People with similar challenges benefit from a community learning experience where they can share experiences and practices on a regular basis.

- The mystery of how to work *smarter*, not just *harder*, has not been adequately addressed in most organizations.

Think for a moment about the type of leadership your organization needs from your operational-level managers these days. Now ask yourself this: "What do I really think the odds are of us consistently getting the performance we are counting on from our operational-level managers without doing things differently?"

If you answered something that approximates "pretty low," then what if…

- you could link managers' problem-solving ability together like computers can be linked for greater processing power?

- management development could become process-driven rather than event-defined?

- development took place in small doses over time, rather than large doses in concentrated time?

- operational-level managers were developed to become the best operational-level managers they could be without concern for upward advancement?

- development and the application of learning took place in a near-real-time experiential environment using actual situations faced?

- managers derived most of their developmental benefit from conversations with other managers facing similar issues?

If these outcomes sound like good value for your organization, you are probably working in an environment similar to most places, meaning that most places would recognize the opportunity being described.

# CHAPTER 2

# RESTORING THE LUSTER TO MIDDLE MANAGEMENT

Distinct from senior/executive levels of management, the operational (senior, middle, or frontline) manager operates much of the time "in the moment," with responsibilities that have immediate and often conflicting deliverables. In many instances, the issues they face cannot be put off without incurring undesirable consequences. The ability of people in these positions to work successfully under conditions of increasing complexity and in the face of often-continuous ambiguity is a requirement of the modern work environment.

Operational-level managers oversee execution in most organizations. They operate on the often-hazy divide between strategic and operations management. They are the source of what the customer identifies as "delivering the goods" in virtually all companies. Their development is, therefore, a strategic concern and critical to the overall needs of the larger organization.

For at least the past two decades, there has been a great deal of attention and allocation of resources aimed at reducing the number of operational-level managers in businesses. This attention and its desired effects have been well intended, yet often misguided. The overarching consequence today is that operational-level and frontline managers have more responsibility and fewer resources with which to achieve results.

Working harder to keep pace with demand has a natural threshold, and quickly reaches a point of diminishing returns as mounting job stress leads to reactionary practices and ill-conceived decision-making. The pressures to reduce expense and increase effectiveness are legitimate; however, the unintended consequence of these practices may, in many ways, offset the benefits achieved. As expectations of operational-level managers continue to expand, these individuals need new thinking. New thoughts will lead to new actions, and managers will become more effective, stronger leaders while fostering greater accountability, responsibility, and inclination to initiate among those employees they manage.

An entirely new intelligence is needed in our organizations to deal with the complexity that now is simply the world of business. This new intelligence will be more community-based; less individual-outcome focused, and be built on the development of powerful working relationships, collaborative skills, and perspectives. This new intelligence has already been distinguished in works such as *Social Intelligence: The New Science of Human Relationships* by Daniel Goleman, *Wired to Connect: Dialogues on Social Intelligence* by Daniel Goleman et al, and *Social Intelligence: The New Science of Success* by Karl Albrecht. The work that has been achieved to understand social intelligence is important. However, the frames of references in which the initial work has developed are either individual or honoring of current hierarchical models. Both represent additive knowledge (incremental improvement) being developed within current constraints rather than launching into entirely new operational constructs that offer the opportunity to generate performance at unprecedented levels. The current set of operational-level management skills and mindset is, for the most part, insufficient to the problems of the 21st century's often ambiguous and always fast-paced business environment. Managers must learn ways to lead more for engagement than compliance. They must delegate, develop, and reward frontline employees, with an eye towards building the capacity of frontline workers to make sound decisions and take effective action from a community perspective in the face of increasingly complex challenges.

# CHAPTER 3

# RECOGNIZING THE POWER IN THE LATERAL CONNECTIONS

How do you tap the "lateral power" in your organization? Maybe you didn't even know it was there!

From the Merriam-Webster Dictionary: **Power**, as a concept, is defined as the capability of acting or of producing an effect.

In physics: **Power** is the rate at which work is performed or energy is converted.

In business: **Power** is the rate at which work is performed and capital and human energy are converted into customers.

From the Merriam-Webster Dictionary: **Lateral** is defined as relating to, characteristic of, or borne upon the side of any object.

In business, *lateral power* then is that latent capability in an organization that is tapped when functional priorities are aligned *laterally* towards accomplishment of clearly understood and defined mutual objectives. This *lateral* alignment of functional priorities frees up human resources, otherwise constrained in service of hierarchical concerns, to engage more completely with the creation and retention of customers.

There are a lot of things in life that we don't see until they are named or distinguished for us. In organizational life, "lateral power" may well be one of these things. To be certain, we have from time to time tapped into the lateral power grid. The organization's hierarchy that has its own forceful, frequently unconscious and unintentionally suppressive nature mostly hides it. Usually, lateral power becomes visible around some sort of crisis and, when it does, we call it *teamwork*, a term that does not capture the full opportunity available.

We are all very familiar with the concept or ideal of teams and teamwork. Depending on our industry, software or hardware development for instance, working in teams to deliver our products is the way the work gets done; it is the *only* way things get done given the complexity of the tasks.

But how about in those very same companies, or others, where *team* is more a label than a fact, as when we refer to the "leadership team," the "executive team," or the "management team?" Are those really teams, or terms we use to identify certain parts of the organizational hierarchy? Do those teams really demonstrate "lateral power," or do they fit Webster's general definition of team: *a number of persons associated together in work or activity?*

Do these types of teams in your organization function like collaborative communities, or a *number of persons associated together in work or activity?*

## SEARCHING FOR UNTAPPED POWER SOURCES

Contrast the following description of a team designed to optimize lateral power and organizational learning with what you might experience or witness in your own organization…

> Imagine a school superintendent's or a CEO's leadership team that meets regularly for getting work done and can be counted on to consistently drive the organization toward the accomplishment of its goals. Much of the time it carries on in straight-ahead work mode, just as it always has, but with a significantly greater level of effectiveness than might normally be expected with a group like this.

Does this sound like your leadership team, or any of your teams? Or does this sound like a description of the way you hope your teams would function? If this sounds like a description of a dream team that has solved the riddle of working smarter rather than working harder (consistently driving toward the accomplishment of its goals!), you have drawn the right conclusion. But now you are going to ask, "How did they get smarter?" They've tapped into lateral power.

The first question, "How did they get smarter?" is not a trick question or based in deception. No, it is a tough question; a question which has not been adequately answered though employers have invested significant energy and dollars to pursue improvements in the level of employee engagement and performance over the past decade. Engagement is a key element in the answer, but we seem to still be a long way from understanding how to enable this condition, especially given the diversity of our workforces. The very same employers that are desperately pursuing engagement are still not tapping the lateral power grid, mainly because it is hidden behind all the concerns for maintaining hierarchical propriety and perpetuating the limitations of current modes of employee development.

Now, here is the answer to the question of how this team got smarter from the source that asked it...

*"It is because the team has also developed a robust and continually accessible second channel. At regularly scheduled intervals, and spontaneously when the need arises, it can shift from an operational to a learning mode. Team members are aware of their own and others' resistance or immunities to change, and of the group's collective tendencies to protect itself from the very progress it seeks to make."[2]*

These folks are plugged in to lateral power. How did they get there? How do they stay there?

They engage in facilitated practice: regularly, consistently, and whole-heartedly. They also do not differentiate between work and development; because, for this team, development is work and work is development. There is no separation.

We have all been in this situation; the stakes are clear; the talent is available; and suddenly, at the most crucial of times, we meet the enemy…and it is us! Only, unlike the dream team being described here, we cannot get out of our own way, or when we do, either in part or grudgingly, the work gets done but at a dear price, and the future looks like a steeper climb. No one is really looking forward to the next time we get together.

# CHAPTER 4

# THERE ARE TWO ROADS

## THE ROAD WELL TRAVELED

In today's business environment, the language of "growth" and "development" is widespread; everyone on their own struggling or underperforming team may have even participated in their company's "university." So, what gives? We have all completed the leadership or management development curriculum, so why are we struggling? Why don't we shift back and forth from operating to learning mode like the "dream team" described earlier? Where is the pathway forward to access lateral power?

Chances are good that, in our corporate university, we were exposed to the traditional *"transmission model"* of adult education. This format rests on the premise that a subject matter expert can transfer crucial knowledge to us by some means: lecture, videos, role playing, simulation, etc. The expectation is that the learner has an insufficient store of information, the expert will "add" some of what is missing, and voila! Performance improves. There is no presumption that the learner may already know what to do and, by virtue of other factors, cannot execute on that knowledge. Really! How many times immediately after making a mistake have you muttered to yourself, "I know better than that!"? And when this happens, we really did know better. Usually, we have no clue as to how to avoid making the same mistake again because knowledge had nothing to do with the mistake we made. It was what we didn't know that we didn't know tripping us up. And we were not supported by peers to prevent a reoccurrence.

The traditional transmission model assumes perfect ability to apply what is being learned. If not, there must be some defect of character or attitude involved. So, the net difference between our struggling team and the dream team is that we have an attitude problem?

You shouldn't accept this conclusion, so let's go to a road less traveled for some insight.

## THE ROAD LESS TRAVELED

What if one difference between our team and the dream team is that they are better able to distinguish between the types of issues they face? They recognize that there are differences in types of issues, and that these differences call for different approaches. For the sake of this discussion let's say issues fall into two large categories: technical/operational and adaptive. The dream team does a better job than our team at spotting the differences between technical/operational and adaptive issues, and addresses each in a different manner. They have learned these distinctions together as they practice.

Table 1 displays one version of the distinctions between the two big categories.

## TABLE 1: DISTINCTIONS BETWEEN TECHNICAL PROBLEMS AND ADAPTIVE CHALLENGES

| Technical Problems | Adaptive Challenges |
|---|---|
| 1. Easy to identify. | 1. Difficult to identify (easy to deny) |
| 2. Often lend themselves to quick and easy (cut and dried) solutions. | 2. Require changes in values, beliefs, roles, relationships, & approaches in order to work. |
| 3. Often can be solved by an authority or expert. | 3. People with the problem do the work of solving it. |
| 4. Require change in just one or a few places often contained within organizational boundaries. | 4. Require change in numerous places, often crossing organizational boundaries. |
| 5. People are generally receptive to addressing technical problems. | 5. People often resist even acknowledging adaptive challenges. |
| 6. Solutions can often be implemented quickly, even by edict. | 6. "Solutions" require experiments; they can take a long time and cannot be implemented by edict. |

Having taken even a cursory look at this table, you can probably quickly identify that teams often get hung up even acknowledging the "adaptive challenges" they face, much less dealing with them. The dream team, with practice and facilitation, has developed the ability to move fluidly back and forth between the two categories of issues. But who knows, maybe they are just more talented than we are.

Don't accept this conclusion either. Let's continue our journey along this road less traveled.

More likely, the truth of the matter resembles something like this: There is no appreciable difference in the people or talent who populate the dream team, and those on our team. Both teams are made up of dedicated people doing the best they can with the means they have available. The differences lie in the "means available," and a key structural element.

Where the dream team assembles, the company has created a culture with a *developmental stance* towards employees. This is to say that the company expects not only productivity from employees, but also that they will grow as people while employed there. The company is prepared to invest in employee growth.

What does a culture with a *developmental stance* look like?

# CHAPTER 5
# DEVELOPMENT AS CULTURE

In their book *Immunity to Change,* authors Robert Kegan and Lisa Laskow Lahey have identified seven crucial elements of a *developmental stance:*

### TABLE 2: ATTRIBUTES OF A DEVELOPMENTAL CULTURE[3]

1. It recognizes that there is "life after adolescence," that adulthood, too, must be a time for ongoing growth and development.

2. It honors the distinction between technical and adaptive learning agendas.

3. It recognizes and cultivates the individual's intrinsic motivation to grow.

4. It assumes that a change in mindset takes time and is not evenly paced.

5. It recognizes that mindsets shape thinking and feeling, so changing mindsets needs to involve the head and the heart.

6. It recognizes that neither change in mindset nor change in behavior alone leads to transformation, but that each must be employed to bring about the other.

7. It provides safety for people to take the kinds of risks inherent in changing their minds.

Having noted these seven elements, you can contrast to your own culture. If, for example, you look at the way you conduct your developmental activities, here's what you'll likely find:

Development is done...

- away from the workplace, classroom focus

- on a periodic event basis

- with the assumption that development is learning, meaning you focus primarily on providing new information

- by centering on individual rather than group learning process, with most classes made up of participants who share no interdependency

- while assuming all developmental issues to be more or less technical, developing skills is sufficient

While your current approach may be sound for technical issues, it is based on a model of education designed for children and carried over into your workplace. Fortunately for you, the model will suffice for technical education, but it falls short of what the *dream team* has been exposed to in their environment with a strong *developmental stance*. Here is a list of differences between your approach and the one over where the *dream team* operates.

## TABLE 3: DESIGN FEATURES FOR ORGANIZATIONAL LEARNING[5]

| Skill Development Focus | Outcome Focus |
| --- | --- |
| 1. Learning in artificial groups (classes) | 1. Learning in real work groups |
| 2. "Time out" apart from work flow | 2. Infusing learning with work flow |
| 3. Time-limited | 3. Time elastic |
| 4. Indirect learner accountability | 4. Direct learner accountability |
| 5. Informational/technical | 5. Transformational/adaptive |
| 6. Seeking transfer of learning | 6. Starts at transfer of learning |
| 7. Serving team-leaders | 7. Co-teaching with team leaders |
| 8. Tight boundary between learning boundaries/adjunct faculty personnel and line personnel | 8. Loose |
| 9. Loose connections to overall corporate strategy | 9. Tight connection to strategy |
| 10. In preparation for an initiative | 10. In support during/continuously |

Perhaps in reviewing the differences in developmental environments, you can see that if all you faced were technical challenges, you'd be fine. However, your employees are a group of adults faced with complex issues; some technical, some adaptive, and you are not preparing them well for the latter. By the way, the *dream team's* developmental environment includes both sides of the table above. The primary difference you'd see if you visited their environment is that much of the developmental education is woven into the work flow in real time, and takes place in intact team sessions with the aid of facilitators and guest experts. You can also very likely see why the dream team's environment reflects the road less traveled.

For at least the better part of a century, we've been using an educational design crafted from the command and control mode. For a certain time and an economic reality, it worked, but that time is now gone and the world of distributed leadership and decision-making is upon us. We have all reached the end of that road we traveled for so long.

Before moving on, consider this. An attempt is being made here to establish that access to lateral power is not gained by participation in a traditional developmental event or experience. Lateral power is developed through participation in a "distributed developmental community" (DDC). It is distinguished as an opportunity in a developmental environment. The process of distinguishing the opportunity of lateral power will be compelling, but alone it will be insufficient to sustain the access. You must be continuingly prepared to constrain the forces that will ask, "Is it over yet? When can we go back to doing things normally?"

Establishing and maintaining a distributed developmental environment based on the belief that there is always room for all employees to grow will threaten the prevailing hierarchy and many an entrenched internal development staff.

- It will test many of the management's large assumptions upon which past practices have been based.

- It will not eliminate the transmission model of education; it will compliment and empower that model.

- It will expand the world of employee development by moving the opportunity right into the place where it can make the biggest difference and offering it when it can make the greatest contribution.

## AN OUTCOME-DRIVEN PRACTICE

You cannot take employee development directly into the day-to-day workplace and not have it become outcome driven. The environment itself will shout the question, and rightly so, "How is this going to help us produce the results?"

What you will find when adding the element of adaptive development into the direct working environment is that teams of employees or managers, *"…will prefer programs that 'start at transfer'—designs that are rooted within real, intact operational workgroups. In these groups the members have a purpose and mission beyond their collective learning, to which that learning is tightly linked. Because they work at real challenges together every day, they naturally have a continuing and self-interested need to see change and improvement in each of their colleagues, and are automatically inclined to appreciate it when it occurs."[5]*

# PART 2

## MAKING THE CASE FOR THE DISTRIBUTED DEVELOPMENTAL COMMUNITY (DDC)

# CAPITALIZING ON INTERDEPENDENCY

The Developmental Community is an idea that has been around in various forms for many years. Historically, its near approximation may be the "community of interest" or "community of practice," though both types of interest group focus primarily on something they do in common for which they have a passion. In this case, the "Distributed" aspect is one feature that makes it unique. Since development in its various formats has historically been centralized, the idea of distributing development takes it out of a framework where it can be considered extra to the work of the organization. I contend that development of employees, in this case mid-level managers, in the environment where the work of the organization takes place, is essential, strategic, and non-optional in the modern business world.

The labor market is awash with open positions; talented people have never been more mobile. If a business is going to be able to both recruit and retain the talent it needs, there must be a robust and vibrant developmental stance within an enterprise that is palpable and observable on a daily basis. Work practices must include developmental activities as regular routine.

Distributed Development then becomes a term of art used when referring to the practices of carrying on development as "the work" of the enterprise, not extra to it and therefore optional. Distributed Development is also then used in a context where the responsibility and opportunity for development are synonymous and take place within the fabric of the work being performed.

The truly unique feature of the Distributed Development Community is its nature. Each community—and there can be as many as serves the organization—is an ongoing occasion to participate in a developmental activity in full partnership with others who are truly committed to your success as an investment in their own success. This means that the ideal Distributed Development Community is populated with members who are obviously and measurably interdependent as a critical element of successfully fulfilling their accountability.

What follows is a story. I've chosen the story format because it has proven over the past 10 years to be both popular and effective in allowing readers to engage a variety of

> "EACH COMMUNITY—AND THERE CAN BE AS MANY AS SERVES THE ORGANIZATION—IS AN ONGOING OCCASION TO PARTICIPATE IN A DEVELOPMENTAL ACTIVITY IN FULL PARTNERSHIP WITH OTHERS WHO ARE TRULY COMMITTED TO YOUR SUCCESS AS AN INVESTMENT IN THEIR OWN SUCCESS."

concepts at an emotional level. It has been well established in many other publications, such as *Switch: How to Change Things When Change is Hard* by Chip and Dan Heath, that an emotional connection is the prime mover of behavioral change. The story creates the emotional connection to allow for proposed changes to take root in the most rapid fashion possible. Make no mistake about it; while the notion of a Distributed Developmental Community will "make sense" to many, if not all, managers, full participation comes about because of making an emotional connection to the practice.

# CHAPTER 6
# THE STORY OF MONEYPUMP

My name is Ron Wallace. I am a department manager at MoneyPump, a national provider of financial services. We are also an insurer, so we're the backer of many of the products we offer. It's a bit tricky, but we try not to compete with the companies whose products we broker. After 45 years in business, we still don't always get it right. I am sure you understand.

Of all the responsibilities I have as a manager, probably the one that gives me the most trouble is the budget process; not the managing of it, the projections. I truly find it hard to know 90–180–365 days ahead what we'll need and what we'll spend. And honestly, I hate making the budget more important than what the moment seems to require. I have been at the process of developing the budget for next year since 6:30 a.m. today, and I see no light at the end of the tunnel.

As I start on the next section, I become aware that there is someone standing in my doorway. Just what I need, an interruption. I knew I should have worked on this at home! "Got a minute?" These words from Carolyn Duncan make this sound like a request but her tone indicates something a bit stronger.

I've known Carolyn for several years; she leads a part of the business that my group really counts on. For the past year we've had our challenges getting what we need from her people. At the moment, I am hoping this is not going to be a request for me to get involved in some sort of political tug-of-war with managers from our respective groups.

"Yeah sure Carolyn, come in and sit down." I am pretty sure my lack of enthusiasm is poorly disguised in my response.

"Carolyn, you look like someone shot your dog. I hope whatever this is isn't that serious."

"Ron, I'm not a dog owner so I don't know if this is THAT serious." She smiles briefly and continues, "I'll let you tell me after we talk a while."

With that, Carolyn sits straight up in her seat and begins. "I have had enough of something, and I want to ask for your help." Without further explanation, I have no way of knowing whether this mention of needing my help is good or bad news, but we're into it now; I was the one who asked her in.

"What exactly is it that you've had enough of, Carolyn?"

"I hate to admit it, Ron, but I have had enough of my managers coming to me with excuses about how we miss our deliverables because some other group doesn't cooperate with them. Sometimes the complaints are about your people, and sometimes they are about Sheryl Hughes' group, but one thing is constant; it isn't them who are at fault. At first I thought what they needed was for me to run interference for them, set up treaties of cooperation between groups like yours and ours on their behalf. You probably remember we did that a couple of times. Honestly, I know you've addressed the issue with your folks, and I believe you have been sincere in your dealings with me."

Carolyn continues, "I took over this group 18 months ago and the excuses started almost immediately. Our performance is not terrible, but it is certainly subject to criticism and, in my opinion, could be much better. From past experience, I'd know exactly what to do; address the issue within my own group and train, move, or remove people if we couldn't get the performance we needed. This is the first time I have had an assignment where so many of our results were dependent on people outside my direct span of control. Quite frankly, I did not know what to expect, but I didn't realize that relying on other groups would be the equivalent of flying blind."

I pipe in at that point, "So, is the situation urgent in your mind?"

She doesn't hesitate. "If by urgent you mean that we've got some customers who are losing patience with us, then I say it is!"

So there it is. I can immediately see that I am not going to finish my budget today. I have to be honest, when I am faced with an apparent choice of addressing customer needs or making my senior management happy, I can be counted on to opt for whatever I see is in the customer's interest. I've been told on several occasions that this particular "quirk" of mine is keeping me from serious consideration for higher-level positions. Just between us, I'll tell you a secret. I know that and it doesn't affect my choices. I know who I am. I know what I am good at. My group's results are always at or above expectation, and honestly, I am not looking to get promoted. I am best suited to be a mid-level manager and damn valuable to this company right where I am!

I love operations management. I love managing in the middle of it all, it satisfies me financially, and, as importantly, it gives me the opportunity to do what I love most: develop people to their full potential. And we do good work to boot! Right now, I manage managers who manage people who deliver service to our clients. That's really as far up the pyramid as I want to go; another step up and there would be too many layers between the customer and me. Worse, I'd be cut off even further from the day-to-day interactions I have with the folks who serve the customers directly.

This story is about that idea: knowing yourself well enough to be confident of where you fit in with the organization you are currently employed by. It is also about coming to grips with the mindset held by many senior as well as middle managers; that being in the middle as a manager is somehow an indication that you were not good enough to move up, or that you lack the ambition to go further. Maybe, like me, you'll come to believe that managing in the middle is a legitimate career destination, a place where those who want to manage and have a distinct set of talents and values find themselves most at home. Their "sweet spot" is what it might be referred to. But it is also about how to leverage the opportunity of "living" in the middle of an organization. If that is where you are now and, like me, you know for whatever reason, "gut instinct," past experience, or personal goals, that it is the right place for you, then the story that follows holds something important.

Each chapter will be a continuation of the adventure Carolyn and I are about to begin. Along the way, we'll meet other managers, some like Carolyn or me, passionate about both customer service and employee development. Some of the people we'll meet have a passion for one or the other and we'll see how it affects the way they manage. One manager in particular, Beverly Martinez (Bev), will prove to be a big surprise as we'll find that she has already begun to address the issue Carolyn and I are facing, and was just about to ask us to join her in a larger experiment. We'll meet Bev in the next chapter.

As the story unfolds, you'll be introduced to some new concepts. Actually, you may find that the concepts are not as new as the names we've given them and the way they have been organized. Some of what you read will verify your instincts and provide a vocabulary that you can use to let other people know what you are doing and get them to join with you.

There are two primary takeaways from the story, and there may be more—but that will be for you to determine for yourself. The first is that, as managers, whether in the middle or otherwise, we've reached a point in this global economy where we have no choice but to de-trivialize the notion that we must "work smarter, not harder." I know this admonition has been popular in American business since the early 1960s. For me, it has often felt like an Aikido move used by senior managers to respond to the challenges that often arise following a force reduction; not accompanied by a "work that needs to get done" reduction, as in, "Well gang, I guess we are just going to have to work smarter, not harder." That has never felt good to me. I looked into the origins of this familiar motto, and find at best it is ascribed loosely to those of Scottish heritage, but more specifically to Scrooge McDuck. He is of Scottish origin himself, of course! Scrooge McDuck and this motto first appeared in print in 1947. Scrooge, of course, never met a worker he didn't despise, so while it may not be meant to have manipulative undertones, the motto is at least somewhat suspect.

Kidding aside for the moment, it was probably Alan Lakein's book, *How to Get Control of Your Time and Your Life*, published in the mid-1970s, that began to make the notion popular, if not merely handy. However, in my mind, most discussions I have participated in on this topic have been cosmetic. Sincere, but cosmetic nonetheless in that they didn't lead to any breakthroughs, and then we went right back to working harder—much harder.

The second major takeaway is this: Carefully crafted collaboration paired with deliberate development is likely the answer to the "work smarter" question. This notion, too, can be trivialized; of course we need to collaborate with others in the workplace. However, the kind of collaboration that will result in the type of smarter work that will keep you coming back for more requires deep thinking and a kind of focus most of us are not well prepared for. For the most part, we treat our working relationships in a transactional manner, and do not effectively distinguish between the friends we have in the workplace and the collaborators. We also, whether we realize it or not, operate from the belief that "smart" means IQ smart. In our story, we are going to challenge that notion and ask you to consider adopting a definition of "smart" in an organizational setting that is a combination of IQ and psychological/emotional maturity.

Unless we confront the hard work of learning how to establish the kinds of working relationships that will yield the collaboration we need, then the thought is just one more wishful slogan. There is a discipline to developing powerful collaborative relationships. You may have figured this out for yourself, but in our story, you'll be introduced to a vocabulary and a set of distinctions that will enhance your capability to collaborate no matter what stage you are at.

That's enough background for now, Carolyn and I are already on our way down the hall to see if we can find Sheryl Hughes.

# CHAPTER 7

# THE STORY IMMEDIATELY TAKES A TURN

As Carolyn and I advance down the hallway, it occurs to me that I am not exactly clear on what we are so hotly pursuing. Yes, Carolyn had used the magic words 'client and unhappy' with me, which got me out of my chair. I know Sheryl's group is intertwined with both Carolyn's and mine in terms of delivering service, so it makes vague sense that we are on our way to talk with her. What I am not clear on is what we are going to do once we find Sheryl. Launching into an "ain't it awful" tirade at 8:30 a.m. on a Tuesday unannounced does not seem like the most productive approach, no matter what we are aiming for.

"Hold on a moment Carolyn, can we just stop in the cafeteria for a few minutes and get clear about what we'll be asking Sheryl about, or telling her about, or whatever we are going to talk with her about?"

Carolyn pulls up from her head-down plunge mode, and looks at me with a puzzled expression. "Well I thought I made that clear back in your office."

"No, Carolyn, what you actually made clear was you were fed up with your people making excuses for not delivering. You didn't say it was my problem too, but somehow here I am on my way to see Sheryl, and I am not yet clear about what you want from me. You may be clear but I am not, and I need this conversation."

So, we head into the cafeteria, grab coffees, and find a table away from everyone else near the windows overlooking the parking lot. Nice view. No wonder the tables were empty!

"So, what do you want from me, Carolyn?"

"Ok, now that we are sitting here, I can actually see that I am not sure what I wanted when I showed up at your office a few minutes ago. I know for sure that I was very upset, but honestly, I don't even remember thinking, 'Oh, I need to talk with Ron; he'll know what to do.' I think it was just more that when I found this morning that another one of my expectations had not been met, I sort of knee jerked out of my chair and the next thing I knew, I was in your doorway!"

"Good, then let's take the time like I suggested and get as clear as we can before we involve Sheryl."

Carolyn stares out the window for nearly a minute, then turns to look at me. "I don't know. Hard as it is to own up to, I don't know what to do, and arriving at your office was an act of sheer frustration."

I figure that has to be a tough admission for Carolyn; she has a reputation for always getting the job done. This new assignment is definitely more complex than anything she has faced, and she did inherit a situation that had been allowed to get out of hand. Still, none of the senior management is interested in hearing excuses from her.

"If you don't know what to do and you wanted to see whether you'd burst into flames by admitting it, you came to the right guy. You may have worked with and around people who insist on the pretense of knowing, but with me, you have found an oasis. I eat uncertainty for breakfast!" I say with a straight face, then burst into laughter. "C'mon, Carolyn, I know you think some clients are at risk, and maybe they are, but we can probably fix that with a few phone calls to the right people. The bigger issue is, what can we do to address the tradition of excuse-making that has infected your group? And by the way, we catch that bug from time to time in my group. Nasty business!"

Carolyn smiles just a crack. "If there is one thing I am not comfortable with, it is feeling incompetent; actually the only thing that even approaches bothering me more is whining! How am I doing?" With this admission, she seems to lighten just a bit.

"So why were you on your way to see Sheryl then?" I ask.

Carolyn pauses and then, looking sheepish, she says, "Honestly, Ron, it was probably more knee jerking on my part. I know how sensitive you are to client issues, so I see now that I used that to suck you in. I apologize."

I opened my arms wide and sat back. "No need to apologize to me. I am as human as the next person. Sometimes the unworkability around me just takes over and my head feels like it must be the inside of a beehive, just buzzing. When I get that way I often find myself searching out Bev Martinez over in Customer Experience. She has always been a good sounding board for me, and she seems to see right through me if I try to play victim with her. I think, in this case, she might be good counsel for you since her group is not intertwined with yours for anything. Have you met her?"

Carolyn looks at me with what I think is skepticism, "I have heard her name, always mentioned in a positive way, but we've never met. What makes you think she can help since she is not involved?"

"Bev is a terrific manager; in fact, I say she is a manager's manager. There are a lot of people who owe where they are now to having spent some time working under her guidance."

"If she is such a terrific manager, why hasn't she been promoted? From what I hear, she has been in her current position for about seven years, and that sounds like she has hit a dead end." This remark comes out of Carolyn's mouth as much of a knee jerk response as showing up in my office.

I stand to leave. "Okay," I say, "Based on that comment I am now very sure that Bev is someone you'll benefit from knowing. She has not been passed over for promotion; she has made it clear that her current role is one she'd like to continue to play for a number of years. She thrives on developing managers, and with the growth in her area, she has frequent opportunities to work with new people. Take a look at promotions or transfers out of her group last year. You'll see that she regularly turns over 30–40 percent of her group. Managers in her group are in high demand and, if you look at job postings, you'll always see vacancies in her shop. Normally, senior management would be asking what's the problem, why the turnover? In Bev's case, several of the senior managers worked under Bev's oversight for a while, and they know exactly what the turnover means. Success!"

"It has been probably 10 months since I've seen her in person. We talk frequently, but you know how it is; it's a big campus. She normally doesn't schedule meetings until around 10 a.m., so let's stretch our legs and see if she can make some time for us. It is about a 15-minute walk to the building where Bev's office is located, so we better get going."

—

"If she is such a terrific manager, why hasn't she been promoted?"

Classic! Carolyn's almost-automatic assessment of Bev Martinez is an example of a couple of things. Firstly, many managers both in the middle and senior levels see the workplace as an arena where they are competing with other managers for the next level on the career ladder. For them, this is no doubt true. But they may be so focused on the competition that they don't recognize that not everyone is in the same game. Carolyn has been playing the competitive game since she joined the company, and seems to naturally evaluate other managers on this basis—even those she hasn't met. I guess it's a good thing she doesn't know I've been in my position for six years and have no interest in moving up. She may not have been seeking out my counsel!

Secondly, given the competitive perspective of many managers, they are always looking for an edge when interacting with peers. They see the world through a set of lenses that might be referred to as Win/Lose, and they keep score, not in a ledger but certainly in their heads. Carolyn hasn't even met Bev, but by suggesting she is someone who has something to offer us, I have opened the competitive gates in her mind. As a true competitor, Carolyn instinctively begins the competition even before she has met Bev.

The Us vs. Them illusion permeates the modern workplace as such, simply because it is inherently human to see others as "not you," and as any particular aspect of organizational design. Although, let's be honest, the functional divides that characterize traditional organizational design do more to exacerbate this human habitual inclination than is ultimately helpful. Unless, of course, you intentionally want to create the imaginary silos that so often pepper any conversation about why things aren't working in any workplace.

Inventing and installing structures to intervene in this natural tendency is inspired by the recognition that the organizational structures developed to promote command and compliance have limited value in many modern workplaces, and maybe never really had much to do with getting the work done. When we meet Beverly Martinez, we'll find a manager who has seen past the illusion and initiated a process that just made sense to her. We'll also meet someone who sees that outcomes are produced organizationally as much through relationship as they are through knowledge. Carolyn's introduction to Bev will prove a turning point in her working career, as well as her perspective as a manager of managers.

# CHAPTER 8

# MIDDLE MANAGEMENT AS A CAREER DESTINATION

"So, Ron, what else can you tell me about Beverly?" Carolyn asks as we speed walk our way across the campus.

"Bev," I say. "Everyone calls her Bev. I think you'll like her immediately, but she can be a bit disarming. I think a lot of people have underestimated her over the years and then been surprised later. Bev either has no ego, or she is just so at peace with herself that she has no need to compete with anybody. She certainly doesn't need to have the last word on any subject."

I offer this last evaluation of Bev for Carolyn's sake. If she goes in with her competitive shields up, it will hinder whatever learning might be gained. I've had enough exchanges with Carolyn to know that she wakes up in the morning feisty and needs to calm down just to come in to work.

"So what's her deal then? If she isn't ambitious, how did she get this far? I mean, she is a director; she must have something on the ball?"

From this comment, I can see that I had not completely soothed Carolyn's competitive instincts.

"Oh, she has a lot on the ball alright. She may be the smartest manager I have ever met."

As she lets my comment sink in, I sense that I am stoking Carolyn's competitive fire rather than quenching it. "Let me explain what I mean by smart. I think there is just plain smart, and then there is manager smart. Bev is manager smart. She may be just plain smart, too, but it is not what sets her apart from other managers I have known."

This statement seems to stop Carolyn in her tracks. She actually stops walking, and it takes me a couple of strides to realize it. "Just plain smart, manager smart…what the heck are you talking about?" She has her hands on her hips now, a sure sign that she is going back towards frustration. She trots quickly to catch up and we continue on our way.

"Just plain smart, like IQ smart, that's what I mean by just plain smart. I find it unfortunate that many managers actually compete intellectually with their reports; maybe they just feel the need to remind themselves that they are just plain smart. They develop various ways of showing folks that they deserve to be the manager by virtue of being the sharpest kid in class. Bev doesn't do that. I think she is probably plenty just plain smart. In fact, I think she is so much just plain smart that she knows she can handle any issue that comes her way. But, she doesn't encourage her folks to bring her issues by showing them how just plain smart she is. In fact, she encourages them to develop their own solutions, try them out, and share their findings.

"Now, rather than have you ask me next what I mean by manager smart, let me just go right ahead and give you my definition. Manager smart is the kind of smart that knows that the manager's job is not to be the person who works the longest hours. I see a lot of managers in their offices well past the agreed-upon end of the workday, not looking too happy about being there.

Carolyn chirps quickly, "But if you see them, you're there too!"

"Yes, on occasion I do work into the evening hours. But when I do, I always see the same people in the office, so I know that, for them, it is habitual. It is the way they work, harder not smarter."

"Ouch!" says Carolyn, "Have you noticed I am one of those staying habitually late?"

"Yes, I have noticed. That's one more reason I think it will be useful for you to talk to Bev. She is one of the hardest working people I have ever known, but she relies more on being manager smart than just plain smart. You'll rarely see her here in the evenings."

Carolyn says nothing for the next few moments. We arrive at our destination and, before we even reach the escalator to the second level, I hear someone shout my name, "Ron."

I turn in the direction of the shout, and standing there with arms wide open is Bev Martinez. She continues in a loud voice, "What brings you over to this side of the campus? I didn't think you could get out of your office for coffee, much less a visit to the other side of the MoneyPump world."

As I advance towards Bev, I realize that Carolyn is no longer beside me. I looked back over my shoulder and she is standing at the foot of the escalator. No doubt she is shocked that someone has shouted in the lobby of the MoneyPump headquarters building, and is probably trying to make up her mind about letting it be known that she might be associated with this noisy person.

"You been giving yourself a hard time again, Ron?" Bev asks with a smile; she knows me well, and many of our past conversations have revolved around me getting in my own way and her helping me see my way out.

"Not too much recently, Sister Beverly, but I have found someone who has a lot in common with me and thought she might benefit from spending some time with you." Bev has always made it clear to me that anyone at MoneyPump who needs her help is welcome to ask, no matter where they work in the company.

Bev steps towards Carolyn, who is now looking somewhat sheepish following my less-than-encouraging introduction. "Alright, you can stop with the Sister Beverly stuff." Bev is looking right at Carolyn as she continues to speak with her hand extended. "I have worked hard to help this guy with his manners, but I can see he has been backsliding. Hi, I'm Bev Martinez; I don't believe we've met."

As Carolyn will soon find out, being noisy is the least surprising thing about Beverly Martinez. Carolyn Duncan is in for a truly eye-opening experience. She is about to have an audience with the managers' manager, and she really isn't ready for what she will learn.

# CHAPTER 9
# ACKNOWLEDGING THE PROBLEM IS THE FIRST STEP TOWARDS A BREAKTHROUGH

*I am betting you didn't read this chapter heading and then say to yourself, "Acknowledge the problem! Oh, my, that is a startling concept I haven't heard before." To the contrary, like a lot of things in life, we usually…*

- know what to do

- know what not to do

- maybe even know who to talk to or ask for help

But how many times, right after you have done something you knew better than to do, have you said to yourself, "I know better than that"?

My first guess is that you have said these words to yourself at least several hundred times—or you lead a really boring life.

Knowledge confers no ability, and it certainly does not predict behavior. What you are going to read about in the following pages is the value in not simply acknowledging that you have a problem, but doing so publicly, and more importantly, doing so in the form of a request for assistance, coaching, or help. The act of authentically acknowledging responsibility for an existing problem, as well as asking for help, shifts your relationship to the problem. First, you make the problem visible to yourself, then to someone else along with a request for help. In doing so, you set up a condition of implied accountability. You have made yourself available to be held to account for resolving your own problem. Nice going!

—

Bev ushers us up to her office. Before she sits down with us, she asks her assistant to move a couple of meetings scheduled shortly to later in the week, commenting to us, "That's tactical stuff I just moved, sounds like what you have brought me may be a bit more strategic."

Carolyn looks at me, then back to Bev, "I don't know if it's that important, Bev. I am having some challenges with my team's performance, which I am hoping you can give me some tips on. Ron speaks very highly of you and your reputation. Even before today, he has always had me interested in meeting you."

"So, if I am so interesting," Bev responds, "Why haven't we met before today, Carolyn? Let me guess; you have never been at the point where you felt the need to reach out for help, or maybe were willing to admit it. That's one of the things that makes me crazy about working here; everybody waits until they have a crisis before they reach out or seek out other managers that might be valuable connections for them."

By the time she finishes her sentence, Bev is on her feet and heading towards the whiteboard in her office.

"Look!" She is almost shouting. She starts drawing something that resembles a wedding cake. She turns and shakes the dry erase marker right at us. "We measure so much individual performance around here. No one, especially a manager, wants to own up to the reality that this place and our business have become so complex that it is really hard to know who should get credited for which results. We are so concerned about annual reviews and evaluations, which, by the way, everybody cheats on, that we completely underutilize the talents of our most valuable people—our mid-level managers. I don't mean that individually they are the most valuable—a lot of them are pretty average folks—but taken as a whole, they represent the most powerful and underutilized asset we have at MoneyPump."

Bev is sort of ranting. Not with an edge, but with a passion that seems to have been pent up for a while. "So, what's with the drawing?" I ask, mainly to slow her down.

"Oh," she laughs and grins, "I got so wound up there that I almost forgot where I was going to start. Carolyn, please understand that my little speech has nothing to do with you personally; it is more the culture of managers here that has me wound up. Staring right into the face of a desperate need to work smarter, we all stand around and go, 'Yup, Yup, gotta work smarter,' then we go right back to working harder. Agggghhh! It makes me crazy. We let systems, policies, and practices that were designed for another time dictate how we are going to work, rather than learn from the work itself!"

"Bev?" I chime in again, as she seems about to take off into another rant. "So, what about the model you started to draw?"

"Oh, right," says Bev. "You know what, Carolyn? I've known Ron for any number of years and I always tell him to loosen up and have a little more fun, show some passion—but I am glad he is so practical, especially when I get like this. Okay!" She turns back to the board to finish her drawing, but of course keeps right on talking.

"You see, there is no question that, as managers, we get paid to see to it that results get produced, obviously in a lot of different areas. If you ask any manager, that's the answer you'll get. If you ask them how that happens, the conversations starts to get interesting. If you hang in there, eventually you'll get that behaviors produce results and the ability to generate the behaviors comes from the resources available. Every manager thinks that if you give them enough of the right people and a sufficient budget they can get the results they are asked for."

Carolyn chimes in at this point. "Well, so far, Bev, I'd agree with everything you've said, and I am at a point where I am beginning to think I don't have the all the right people, at least as my managers."

"That's perfect!" shouts Bev. "You know your track record, you get the job done, and you get results. So if the results aren't there, it must be either the people or the other resources available that are the problem, right?"

"That's why we are here, Bev. I brought this issue to Ron this morning and he suggested—sort of insisted—that we come over here to see you. I assumed we were going to talk about what to do with my managers since I see no issue with the other resources." Carolyn seems into this conversation now.

"Oh, we'll talk about what to do with your managers alright, but it may not look like what you expected." Bev has a sly grin that I have seen before. Carolyn is slowly walking into Bev's lair. Now I am really interested. What will happen when two of MoneyPump's superheroes cross light sabers?

"So, there you are, a manager with a proven track record given a big opportunity to turn around a department with dismal performance for a couple of years, and all that stands in your way are your own people. Is that pretty much it then?" Bev is standing now with her hands on her hips, and this sounds to me almost like an accusation.

"Well that sounds sort of whiny, I'd say." Carolyn is up now, too, and she is leaning with her hands on the chair back. "I certainly didn't mean it to sound that way, but I can see your point. I have gotten myself a bit wrapped around my own axle and maybe I am not disguising my frustration very well. But let me ask you this, what else am I supposed to think?"

Ah, the first sign of vulnerability! Maybe this isn't going to be a bloody battle after all. Bev wisely lets the silence linger. After what seems like five minutes, Carolyn continues.

"Bev, I notice you haven't completed your drawing quite yet. As I am standing here cooking in my own juice, I am beginning to suspect you are going to tell me there is something more to the picture than my stellar track record and my underperforming managers, and I haven't seen it yet. Am I getting warmer?"

Bev quickly turns and now fills in the rest of the drawing, then steps away from the board. "I can see why you have such a terrific reputation, Carolyn. Many managers in your position would have bristled pretty hard at the remark I made and some would have walked out of the office, but you heard what I said and used it to reflect on your own point of view and consider that you might be limiting yourself. That's pretty unusual in my experience."

## Theory of Outcomes in Organizations

"Thanks for the encouragement, Bev, but as you can see, I am in too much confusion about what to do to be getting my back up about much of anything right now. I am really feeling the need for answers and I hope you have them." Carolyn's shoulders drop and she returns to her seat.

"Before I explain the rest of the drawing I want to underscore what just occurred here between the two of us, maybe the three of us—if you'll indulge me. You came in here maybe 30 minutes ago and I expected that you were looking to pose your question and receive an answer, 'Badda bing badda boom! Gotta go now, thank you.'"

Carolyn nods slowly at Bev's statement.

"That is a typical posture, and appropriate in many of the exchanges we have with each other day in and day out. This was going to be a simple transaction. Like a good manager, you were going to admit you have a problem, acknowledge that what you were doing wasn't working, ask for help, and then take your answer back and see if you could apply it." With this, Bev stops for a moment.

Again, Carolyn nods, only now she seems a bit impatient.

"You were going to be the same person when you left as you were when you came in! Am I right?"

Carolyn's eyes widen. "I hadn't really thought much about myself coming in, to tell you the truth. Is that what I missed?"

Bev comes back to her desk now and sits down. "It is some of what you missed, but not all. What I have learned in dealing with problems myself is that they always have something to do with me, and I don't mean just what I am doing. They have something to do with what I am seeing or not seeing about the problem."

This was the magic that I was hoping Bev would begin to share with Carolyn and the primary reason I had brought her to this meeting. I know that, left to her own devices, Carolyn, smart and determined as she is, would have found a solution to her frustration. Unfortunately, there may have been some unintended consequences resulting from whatever solution she would have developed, and it would have likely come from continuing to work harder. From my own experience, I knew Bev wouldn't let her take that route unless she was just too stubborn to listen.

Bev is back on her feet and heading towards the board again. "Carolyn, would you say you fall into the category of managers who think that if they just have sufficient budget and the right people reporting to them that they'll find a way to produce the desired results?"

Carolyn is quick to respond here. "Well, I like to think there is some room in there for my contribution, but essentially yes, I do fall in that category. I don't make excuses; I expect a lot of my people. Once the budget is set we do everything we can to stick to it, and I have always seen to it that the results were produced."

"Until now, that is!" Bev had grabbed a red marker, and is drawing a large egg around the two lower levels of her little wedding cake.

"Until now, you haven't needed to know about these two layers of the cake I have drawn, and I think now is the time to learn. When I suggested earlier that you might need to change, I was referring to something being wrong with the way you were seeing. What I was referring to was simply this: If you arrive at a place where you are presented with a problem and it looks familiar, it stands to reason that you'll attempt to solve it with methods you have previously used successfully."

Carolyn moves to the front edge of her chair. "As a matter of fact, that's a pretty fair statement of what I have been doing. Is that wrong?"

"See how quickly you circle back to assuming there must be something wrong." Bev is now grinning, I know how much she enjoys watching people like Carolyn, and me for that matter, walk themselves right into her invisible learning moments. "What if there is nothing wrong, Carolyn?" she continues. "What if rather than there being something wrong, there is something that you haven't seen, something that was always there but for some reason, maybe good fortune, maybe managers who had done good work before you, whatever, was invisible to you, that either was not required or was so strongly in place that you didn't need to do anything to put it there?"

"Bev, I don't mean to sound rude, but it almost sounds like you are implying that I was just lucky in the past. If that is what you are suggesting, I am going to have trouble accepting that." Carolyn's face is flushed.

Bev bends over, hands on her knees, and laughs a hearty laugh, which I can see catches Carolyn off guard.

As her laughter dies down, Bev speaks again. "No, girl, I would not say you got lucky. Well, maybe, in which case we have all gotten lucky a time or two. No, you just never knew what else there might be that you needed to know. I am not surprised because it doesn't get taught to us in school, and many managers are not able to teach what I am going to simply because they don't know it themselves—which is too bad because it makes us a less effective company. What you have never dealt with before is an insufficient supply of possibility, and I think that is what your main problem is. I am not saying you have all the right people, but before you go there, I'd like you to give what I am talking about a try. It is going to cost you something but not from your budget or your pocket."

"Possibility? If you mean imagination, I have had all I need staring me in the face since I took over this group. These folks have more imagination than I can contend with, and they seem to be experts in using it to create excuses that are bulletproof, at least in their minds." Carolyn's words come with an edge now; her passion is engaged.

"That's not what I mean, and I can see why you'd draw that conclusion as well. No, the possibility I am talking about is more like the room for something to happen. Can you personally think of any time that it looked like something should be able to happen and wasn't happening?"

"Let me think for a minute. While I am thinking, maybe I can calm down a bit too." Carolyn had stood up unconsciously, and walks to the window of Bev's office to gaze out on the lawn. "Okay, let's see if this situation fits your question. A few years ago, my mother and my younger sister had a disagreement about what my sister was going to choose as a major in college. My mother had her heart set on my sister majoring in art, and my sister chose a business major instead. Mom is an artist herself and knows my sister has tremendous talent. She had her sights set for my sister to have a career in the art world. They argued about this so seriously that my mother told my sister she was going to waste her talent, and she refused to pay my sister's college expenses."

I don't know Carolyn well and, as in many cases with people we work with, there is a lot more to know than we see every day in the workplace. This sounds very personal and still a bit touchy as she begins telling the story.

"That was seven years ago, my sister went on to pay for her own college expenses with loans and some grants. My mother stuck to her word and didn't help my sister at all. The consequence that no one in the family expected was that they stopped talking to each other and have not been in the same room since."

I have a feeling that, for Carolyn, the conversation is about to get very real. For a lot of people, this is the kind of thing that they only tell their closest friends. If she is willing to share this type of information with Bev, someone she had met only an hour before, with me present, she must really be playing for keeps with the issues she is faced with, and she must really trust me. This conversation is rapidly taking us into the territory of the soft stuff that is so hard for many of us to deal with in the workplace. But here she is, laying it out for us, leaving room for us to conclude that since she comes from such a dysfunctional family, it is no wonder some sort of problem finally surfaced in her managing style. That is not, of course, what either Bev or I are concluding, but it would have stopped a lot of people I know and work with. At this point I jump in the conversation.

"Carolyn, what did your dad think about all this? I am sure he couldn't have been happy to have your sister and mother not talking to each other."

"I am not sure whether this was part of the issue or not, but my father died suddenly in his early 40s, so he was not around for all this. He left us with some money, but not enough for everything, and Mom needed to go to work. She found herself a position in one of the older companies in our town, and for the next 15 years she set aside her own artistic interests. I know mom felt the responsibility for playing the part of both parents. Knowing that my father had set up college trusts for each of the three kids—I have a brother too—maybe my mother wanted my sister to have an opportunity she felt she had missed." Carolyn is speaking with her back to us, continuing to gaze outside without focus. Clearly, this is a big deal that she is sharing with us.

In the warmest voice I have ever heard coming from her, Bev says to Carolyn, "I am sorry for your loss."

## CHAPTER 10

# IS THAT A LIGHT AT THE END OF THE TUNNEL?

While acknowledging that you have a problem is a necessary first step towards a solution, it is not a solution in itself. It does, however, begin to make possible the solution, which was not the case before the admission. Carolyn is about to find out that learning something you didn't even know was there to be learned is far from a fatal event.

Typically, many work environments unintentionally make the learning that is going to take place for Carolyn next a lot less likely. Practices like evaluating and rewarding performance on an individual basis do not necessarily reveal or emphasize the importance of the collaborative nature of what really makes a difference to any customer or client.

—

Bev lets her words of comfort linger for a few moments. Carolyn says nothing, just returns to her chair. "Carolyn, this is exactly the kind of example I was looking for when I asked the question. Hold on a moment while I arrange for something that I think may move our conversation along." Bev picks up her phone and punches in a few numbers. "Marty," says Bev,

"Could you put your hands on that tea sampler box we have in the break room, fill a carafe with hot water, and bring three cups to my office? Thanks! Oh! Wait another second, is the manager's meeting this morning like it says on the calendar? Okay good, before you bring that other stuff down here, can you stop by that session and let Sonya know I am going to be stopping by in the second half of the session with a couple of guests? Great, see you in a few minutes."

With that, Bev hangs up and turns her attention back to Carolyn and me. "I was feeling like a cup of tea myself. It's all herbal, lots of flavors, fruity, minty, no caffeine. I am assuming this is top priority for you, Carolyn, so I thought we might just as well settle in for the morning. A warm cup of tea always seems right to me mid-morning. Ron, I don't want to assume this has the same priority for you?"

I have been imagining being in Carolyn's chair for many minutes now, recalling some of my sessions with Bev. If this is an invitation, I am not going to miss it. My budget is not due until the following week and this conversation holds the promise of learning something. "You can't get rid of me that easily, Bev; I am not about to leave my friend in your clutches without some sort of chaperone!" We both laugh because, by now, Bev knows from our previous meetings that I would not want to miss what is coming next.

"Alright then!" Bev is back at the board again. "The tea is on the way and a little bit later I'll show you both a live version of a pilot I've been running with managers in our department that I think you'll find very enlightening. In the meantime, let me finally get around to completing this little drawing I was doing by tagging on to the story you told about your sister and your mother.

"You see, Carolyn, in my view, the fact that your sister and mother are not talking is mostly a matter of there being insufficient possibility for them to resolve the issue. From everything I can tell, we actually see similar situations here at work all the time: managers who disagree and stop collaborating, employees who have disagreements and start avoiding each other, managers who have something to say but don't say it. Most of the time, I think these situations get chalked up to people being difficult, personality conflicts, or whatever. Nobody seems to consider that possibly something is not right in the working relationship, which I am going to call CONNECTION because the word seems more active. Some mutual understandings didn't get established, some assumptions have been made. I'll take the example of your mother and sister for a moment to clarify what I am talking about."

Meanwhile, Bev has printed the word POSSIBILITY in one of the remaining open spaces in her drawing.

"Possibility, the room for something to happen, is a function of the CONNECTIONS among people."

Now Bev prints the phrase INHERITED CONNECTION in the remaining space. "Here's what I mean by INHERITED CONNECTION," she says. "It's the natural space available to get work done between people or departments when nothing has been done to design the CONNECTION for what needs to get done. So, you work with what you've got and make the best of it. I came up with this term based on my early working experiences, when I came to MoneyPump naively expecting us to operate like we were all on the same team. Hoo boy, was

I disappointed! It took me a while to realize that, just because the same person signed all our paychecks, did not mean we were on the same team."

"Let me ask you a question," Bev says to Carolyn. "Have you ever had a co-worker or manager act towards you in a way that seemed inappropriate?"

This was the question that eventually led to an eye-opening realization on my part when Bev had this conversation with me.

Carolyn sits up a bit straighter in her chair. "Yes, not very often, but on a couple of occasions. I'll just assume you want an example so I'll mention that a couple of times I have been told jokes by other managers that I thought were in poor taste."

"That is great!" Bev is now using the marker as a pointer again. The cap is off, so I worry that as she waves it around she might graze her own clothes and make a mess in her excitement. "I don't mean great that they told you jokes you thought were inappropriate, I mean great example because it will help me make the point I have in mind. I bet if I asked you if everyone would think the jokes were not appropriate you'd have to stop and think for a moment."

Carolyn raises her eyebrows. "You're right about that. Where are you going with this?"

Bev puts the cap on the marker, so I relax. "Well, not everyone thought the jokes were in poor taste, otherwise whoever told you the joke wouldn't have done that. Does that make sense?"

Carolyn winces. "Yikes, I guess, it seemed to me at the time that the person telling me the joke was just being thoughtless! The jokes that were told to me were inappropriate."

"Well that would mean that inappropriate has an absolute meaning wouldn't it?" Bev tosses this question out almost like a throwaway and then goes silent.

"What do you mean by that, Bev?" Carolyn is wide-eyed now.

"What I mean is that we all assume things, like because we think something is inappropriate, anyone would think it was inappropriate. Sort of stops you cold doesn't it?" Bev's sly grin has returned now. "I am going to say something now that will likely surprise you. The jokes, while I might agree with you and dislike them myself, were not inappropriate. The person telling you the jokes didn't have the type of CONNECTION with you that would allow for those kinds of jokes to be shared with you."

Carolyn pushes herself away from the window sill. "Bev, that sounds like crazy talk. Those jokes were inappropriate. Period. No matter what CONNECTION we had!"

Carolyn has now waltzed herself fully into Bev's trap, and if she listens carefully she might hear the door slamming shut behind her.

Bev turns and puts the marker in the tray below the board. "So, let me ask you this. Have you ever had someone you didn't know very well say something critical to you and you became upset? Of course you have. We all have. Now, have you ever had someone you knew well and trusted say something very similar and you took it in stride? Again, of course you have, as have we all.

"Now I know I am moving a little fast here and the two questions—this one and the other about the jokes—may not seem related, but they are. Think about it for a moment. How is it possible, and I am using the word carefully now, that the very same or similar remarks made by two different people could affect you so differently?"

If Carolyn is anything like me, this question might call for bathroom break. "Okay, I understand the question, Bev, but we've been in here just long enough for me to need a break, so can I answer after a short time out?"

"I'm with you, Carolyn," I offer now. "Can we take maybe 10 minutes, Bev?"

"Sure," says Bev. "That will give me time to check on the session I want us to join to make sure everyone's fine about that."

I can almost read Carolyn's mind at this point. Her antennae are up and all systems are on red alert. There is new information coming, and she isn't sure she is going to like it when it arrives.

# CHAPTER 11
# DOES ANYONE HAVE A WET TOWEL?

As a coach, whether you are interacting with a report or a peer, if you are going to tangle with someone's belief system, you want to make sure they will have a soft landing place available. Bev's set up in this instance is about as gentle as anything I have ever seen. I am very happy I put aside my budget this morning when Carolyn first arrived. She isn't the only one having an awakening here. On previous occasions, I had been in Carolyn's seat; now I am the observer and I can learn for myself how to facilitate this conversation if and when the occasion arises. I was already thinking about who my first victim, err, I mean, subject might be. This sounds terrible, doesn't it?

Look, as an operational-level manager, you are in charge of some of the most precious assets of your company. When I say subject…I mean asset, so let's use that. You are an asset manager and your role is first and foremost asset development.

Carolyn is back now, so the curtain is about to go up on the next act of this play.

—

As she walks back into the office, Carolyn is already talking, "Alright, Bev, I have my answer to your question and I don't like it! If I get what you are driving at—the difference between the comment that I was upset by and the comment I was okay with is the person who made the remark, not necessarily the remark itself. I don't really like the implication of that because it sounds like I am more closed-minded than I realized. I still don't get the connection with the jokes though. They were in terrible taste!"

Bev is reaching for the marker, here we go again! "That's pretty good, Carolyn, you are definitely getting close to my point. How about this? Rather than thinking the difference between the two remarks was the person making them, how about if you considered that it was the CONNECTION or NON-CONNECTION you had with whoever was speaking that made the difference? I mean, the information in both remarks was basically the same, right?"

Carolyn puts her face in her hands for a moment and then sits back. "This seems to be getting worse; am I just dense? Person, relationship, aren't they the same thing? I don't get the difference and I am trying."

"Okay," says Bev. "Just relax, you are not dense. You should have been here when I had this conversation with Ron. I didn't think we were ever going to get out of the swamp!"

"Hey, wait a minute!" I say. "You were just new at all this when you had this conversation with me, Bev. It was like getting a tooth drilled without anesthetic!" I am fine with Bev using me as a foil if it means Carolyn might become a bit less self-critical.

"No, he wasn't that bad and he's right, I was just getting clear about all this myself when Ron and I had that conversation. Fortunately for me, he is too tough to damage."

Bev has her arms folded now. Man, I hope the cap is on that marker or she has a green line under the arm of her jacket!

"Your answer was closer than maybe my question has implied, and the implication you inferred couldn't be further from the truth. In fact, so far from what I have seen, you are very open minded, just a bit foggy like the rest of us. See, from my perspective, there is the person I am interacting with and the CONNECTION I have with them. Anything they say to me has to pass through the filter of the relationship on its way to me hearing it."

Again, Carolyn's eyes get wide, "That must mean they have the same thing going on with you, then. However you respond to them they must pass through their version of a CONNECTION with you, another filter. Yowie, that gets complicated!"

Bev is back to drawing now, "Doesn't get complicated, is complicated. There is no getting complicated, because there is nothing you can do about it except know that it is going on and watch for its effects. Once you get a handle on this concept, you'll see conversations very differently than you ever have. You realize that talk is a precious commodity, and take pains to use it with much greater discretion. I say that because talking is how our relationships get created, and how they become tangled up.

"Did you ever say something to someone and then see their face get sort of twisted for a moment? Of course you have, we all have. That often is a sign of the comment you made trying to find its way through the CONNECTION'S or the filter's pathway. Maybe it doesn't quite fit past patterns, so it has sort of a stone-in-the-hubcap effect, if you know what I mean. You are moving, but there is this awful racket."

"I know exactly what you mean!" Carolyn's face is brightening now, maybe with the light of insight. "Now that you have created that frame for me, I can see that what bothered me about those jokes I was talking about, especially in one case, was that they were inconsistent with my previous experiences. Like I am saying, especially in one case, it seemed way out of character."

I know Bev likes where the conversation is headed now. "Yes, but you didn't know exactly how to feel at the moment of the exchange, right? Here's why: You may have thought the jokes were in poor taste, but based on your previous CONNECTION, one that didn't necessarily include jokes in poor taste, what happened produced a state of confusion. Your own system got jammed, at least for a short time."

"Actually, for a long time; now that we are talking about it, I can see that in one case I didn't have a particularly close CONNECTION with the person telling the joke, so, while I didn't care for the joke, I sort of let it go after a bit. In the other case, it was someone I have been close with and I found that joke so out of character that I have been on guard around him ever since. I haven't known what to think. It has been uncomfortable." Carolyn is glazed over again; I can tell she is right back in that moment, reliving the awkward feeling.

"Yes, we are in the heart of it now. That kind of thing happens all the time, and the mixed feelings you did and maybe are experiencing right now is why people put on their protective shields before they come in from the parking lot each morning. I imagine you put your armor on every morning; most of us do. This is hostile territory. There are hidden snares everywhere and even when we think we can relax a bit, someone tells us a stupid joke or makes some other kind of comment that throws us—maybe it's even just a look on their face. Let's be honest here; the workplace is not the most intimate environment in the world. Everybody is doing their best to imitate machine parts and we hope our gears mesh smoothly. Especially on these days with the increased complexity, it just doesn't work.

"Do you know what the scariest places can be...very successful companies! You might think it would be the other way around, but they can often go one of two ways: people can get careful, no one wants to mess up the success, they fall into deadening routine, the culture becomes super polite, on the surface, and everyone knows what can and can't be talked about. Ugh! We actually were there about 10 years back, but fortunately, new leadership and a sinking stock price helped all that. We needed to be talking about everything; good, bad, and otherwise. It was too bad we had to sink that low, but it was refreshing when the new folks arrived. I actually think that not being able to talk about what needed talking about did more to bring about our slide than anything else.

"The other way successful companies can go is to become tolerant of bad behavior. This would be kind of a cavalier approach. Everything's working, so anything goes. That's not pretty; it can get hostile and success justifies tolerating behavior that everyone knows is out of bounds, but nobody addresses until someone files a law suit. Then everybody acts surprised!"

Bev is really rolling now.

"Okay, let me get down off my soapbox and back to your issue, which is what we need to focus on. So, I think you are starting to see a glimmer of insight here, am I right?"

"What? Oh yes," Carolyn jolts back from her trance. "Sorry if I didn't catch a lot of that last part, but I was paying a visit back to that incident of the joke telling. I caught the last part though, I am seeing a glimmer, but honestly, I am feeling a bit foolish as well. I am a smart person. Why haven't I known this stuff for a while, how come I didn't figure it out on my own before now?"

Bev stares Carolyn right in the eye. "If you had known this, you would be a rare bird indeed. Probably more to the point, you wouldn't be here now and I may not have had the pleasure of meeting you. So, excuse me if I find myself the beneficiary of your ignorance."

CHAPTER 12

# AND NOW FOR MY NEXT TRICK...

I think you can see as this story is unfolding that Bev is both an exceptional person, as well as manager. She has taken Carolyn, a highly regarded employee, and walked her through a major emotional and intellectual learning experience in a remarkably short period of time. Since this is a fable and time is short, it is not possible to cover all possible outcomes to a conversation like the one Bev and Carolyn have been having, but I am sure you can see that it doesn't necessarily always turn out well and, in fact, there can be no guarantee that it will. However, if you consider what is at stake daily in the workplace—not just the financial stakes, which are considerable—but the developmental and even psychological/emotional/spiritual stakes warrant the risk involved in having this type of dialogue.

If you are intrigued thus far, and can see the benefit that Carolyn has already gained by hanging in there with Bev during this dialogue, then I invite you to continue on for what follows: the description of the practical application that Bev developed from her own awakening.

—

Bev is tidying up her desk and shutting down her computer as she continues now. "I can see by your expression, Carolyn, that you are wondering how to respond to my last comment. Don't give it any more thought. It was sincere. I come to work each day for the possibility of having conversations like this with people like you as much as I do for any of the other benefits of being here."

Carolyn reacts to what she thinks Bev is doing as she continues tidying up. "Well, I really appreciate the time, and I have taken up more of both of your days than I had planned. Hopefully you won't mind if I give you a call from time to time, as I see how I can apply what I have learning this morning."

Bev stops what she is doing. "Oh no, my dear, we are not even close to done here. I have meetings scheduled outside the building this afternoon, so I won't be back in here after we leave. I want to get us down to the manager's collaborative session before the opportunity passes. They get together each month for a three-hour session and there's about an hour and a half left now. Seeing this session live will save you and me a lot of conversations in the future. Let's get going so you can see as much as possible. I'll tell you what, you guys go on to the Franklin Conference Room and I'll meet you there. Wait until I arrive to go in; I just want to make the necessary introductions. This is a pretty special space you'll be walking into."

As we head from the conference room, Carolyn is after me immediately. "Ron, who is this woman and why haven't I met her before or heard more about her? She is amazing; I haven't ever gotten this much attention in any of my performance reviews!"

I can't help but smile because I know Carolyn is right about one thing. Bev's name and reputation are not widely recognized, but I also know just a bit about what we are walking into and have a suspicion that Bev is going to become much more well-known at MoneyPump very quickly.

We stop for a brief bathroom break, so by the time we arrive at the conference room Bev is already there. "Hey, I thought I lost you guys, I guess I haven't scared you away yet?"

"No, Bev, we both needed a nature stop; I hope you haven't been waiting long. We are ready for whatever is next." I use my cavalier voice as I complete that last sentence; I really have no idea what to expect next.

As we enter the conference room all heads turn in our direction. "There you are!" A bright smile from across the room greets us. It is from Sonja Anderson, a member of the management development staff at MoneyPump. I've known her for a couple of years and she always seems to have her high beams on. That smile is really something.

"Bev, I'll tell you what, why don't you introduce your associates there and then find seats around the circle? We can squeeze you in if you don't mind being separated and sitting next to strangers. Rather than go through introductions of names you won't remember, we'll just continue our dialogue once you are settled. We're right in the middle of working a problem with Sarah that we've been focused on for about a half hour."

Bev makes the necessary introductions, and we just sort of melt comfortably and silently into the group. The next 90 minutes go by in a blur. I am not sure about Carolyn, but I feel like I am in a dream state—a good dream. What I am witnessing is something I thought only existed in other managers' imaginations. These are cross-functional managers; most of them come from Bev's department—which is large and complex—but not all, and I know from previous conversations that there is some history of frictions when Bev took over here about three years ago. If there had been frictions, they are not in evidence this morning. We are present to an intensely focused dialogue that could be mistaken for a group of friends working to counsel a pal through a death in the family. There is only one laptop in evidence and no cell phones or PDAs, but lots of writing paper and lots of notes hitting the pages. Attention spans remain right on Sarah initially; then, after a brief break, on Sean, another member of the group whose issue wraps up the morning.

Maybe the most compelling part of the interaction is the focused attention and what it seems to provide for the person working their issue. The acceleration in them arriving at an approach they can commit to is palpable in the room. Sonja, as the obvious facilitator, says very little. She seems to be orchestrating the dialogue, as she periodically asks someone who hasn't been heard from in a while to chime in…and they do! Nobody passes up the opportunity to speak. When we arrived, the group had been at this for two hours and, during the time there, no one gave any sign of being in a hurry to finish or leave. In fact, when they finish, they have a catered sack lunch waiting and most of them stay around and talk like best buddies at a pub after work.

I note that there are two types of exchanges that take place. Most often, when speaking to the person working their problem, the group members are asking questions; not lawyer-type leading questions, but authentic questions that seek to learn something about the issue of the problem worker. There are several instances when a member asks the problem worker if they can make a suggestion. They are asking permission!

Usually, the problem worker accepts the request, but not always. A couple of times, the problem worker respectfully declines the request and indicates that they are not quite ready for input at this point. They don't say never, just that the timing is not right. Then, a few minutes later, they might come back to the person they declined earlier and ask them to now make their suggestion. How cool is that? No ruffled feathers, no pouting…just flat-out participation.

Too soon for me, it is time to go. The group asks us to stay for lunch but Bev declines on our behalf. She says she has a meeting outside the building and still needs to finish up with us.

In short order, we are back in Bev's office. Carolyn and I are just jibber jabbering like a couple of magpies while Bev stops briefly to speak with her assistant.

"So you both seem pretty excited." Bev sits down at her desk now, but doesn't have her attention on anything but us.

Carolyn speaks first. "That was real; that wasn't staged. I could tell, but you have to tell me—I mean us, of course— how that kind of collaboration has come about. Those people were locked on that conversation like they had no place else to go, and I know they did. They are managers just like the ones who report to me, and they must have calendars that are just as full."

Bev sits calmly like this was the reaction she had expected from us. "Well, I don't have time to tell you the whole story, which will have to wait for another date if you are willing to come back. I can give you the short version and then I have to go to make that other meeting."

"Can we come back tomorrow? I mean, if that isn't being too pushy. I feel I have a crisis on my hands and I want to get moving fast." Normally Carolyn is one of the coolest customers I know. At the moment though, she is like a little kid anticipating a roller coaster ride, eager and nervous in the same moment.

"If you can wait just a minute I'll check with Marty." With that, Bev grabs her handbag; she is clearly leaving now, but taking just a bit of extra time. She has Carolyn fully hooked at this point—me too, for that matter—she doesn't want to miss this opportunity to get us fully into the boat.

Carolyn is looking me right in the eye now, intently. "Ron, if what we saw today can be duplicated in our groups, then we have some work to do to get something like this started and I want to get Sheryl Hughes involved right away. Do you think we could get her to come back with us tomorrow so she could get the story right from the creator of the approach?"

"Whoa, you are eager. I have some juggling to do myself; I don't want to miss this and I can't speak for Sheryl, but we can drop by her office on the way back to ours and see if she is in a mood to be convinced. I am sure she has other things on her calendar. I'm willing to take the time, so let's do it."

To me, this is the best invitation I've had in a while: the chance to get together with three of my favorite peers on a topic that held a lot of juice for all of us and a lot of upside for MoneyPump. I can work on the budget over the weekend.

Bev steps back into her office doorway. "I can meet with you tomorrow after 2:00 p.m. Does that work?"

Carolyn looks at me. "Well, I can. Ron?"

"I'll make myself available. Bev, we'd also like to bring along one of our peers who has a stake in how this all turns out. I don't want to have you go back through the entire conversation you just had with us. Will that be okay?" I am as eager as Carolyn to get Sheryl Hughes involved but don't want to impose too much on Bev at one time.

"Hmmm, that can be a bit tricky but...here's your chance to see how much of the conversation we had today you have retained. If you can promise me that by 2:00 p.m. tomorrow, you'll have your pal Sheryl up to speed with you and we won't need to backtrack, then yes, she is very welcome. I think we'll need a conference room now that we're having a party, so I'll ask Marty to handle that as I am on my way out. So...?"

Carolyn does not bother to look my way, "I promise Sheryl will be ready to go when we get here!"

"Okay then, see you tomorrow." With that, Bev is out the door.

Carolyn turns to me. "I think we may both have a lot to learn from this lady!"

CHAPTER 13

# THE SORCERESS DOES NOT WEAR FLOWING ROBES

In every place of work, you will find ordinary people producing extraordinary results. If, as you are reading here, you begin to think the people in this story are more talented or smarter than you…stop it!

Carolyn, okay—she is special and will likely move on into senior management within a couple of years. Bev has that kind of talent, but knows where her heart is. She, much like me, derives much of her working satisfaction from seeing those around her perform in ways they had never imagined. Basically, we are ordinary people with a very clear understanding of our talents, and we are powered by what might be considered extraordinary commitments.

—

Poor Sheryl Hughes; she never had a chance. Carolyn and I are so pumped up about both the conversation we'd had with Bev and the group we had seen working together that, when we meet with Sheryl, it is like we are channeling Bev. And Sheryl gets it, even faster than Carolyn and I had. She quickly relates to Carolyn's story about the jokes in poor taste to several of her own experiences. Not only that, she is as eager to address the manager's performance issues in her own department as Carolyn is in her own. Besides, she knows us both, knows neither of us are particularly excitable and, if we are this excited, she wants to come to the party.

As promised, Marty had set up a conference room and is already there when we arrive. He informs us that Bev had asked him to sit in on the session, but wants to make sure it is alright with us. We introduce Sheryl and tell her where Marty fits into the picture. She is fine with the arrangement, so we take our various places around the table.

Bev walks in about a minute early, but begins right away. "Well, it looks like everyone has met, and if Marty is still here, I assume you guys are fine with that?"

We all nod, and I begin by introducing Sheryl to Bev. Bev immediately wants to know if Sheryl has any questions. I suppose she is testing to make sure Carolyn and I have kept our promise.

"I am sure I'll have a lot of questions as we go along, Bev, but nothing that cannot wait until later." From the look on Bev's face it appears that we have passed the challenge that Bev gave us yesterday morning.

"Okay, let's get rolling. Assuming that everyone is planning to leave at 5:00 p.m., we have about three hours—which should be enough time to get done with at least the high-level version of what you were witness to yesterday.

"I think I may have mentioned that this group has been together for about 10 months. It is the product of two other attempts that didn't turn out as well…but we did learn a lot."

My curiosity gets the best of me here. "Bev, I hadn't heard about this group, and certainly didn't hear about the first two attempts. Can you talk about those?"

"Well, Ron, I was going to do exactly that. One thing I think we all need to learn at MoneyPump is that, if we are ever going to be anything other than what we have been, we'll need to take some chances and there will be some failures along the way. And, I think it is very important to recognize failures when they do occur; otherwise, we won't want to spend time learning. This probably all sounds like something I read in a management text, but I can tell you from experience that there is a world of difference between saying the words and being there when things don't work out. It isn't that there were any grand tragedies along the way; it's just that, without those first two attempts, I doubt we'd be where we are today. So, what I want to underscore is the necessity of doing something different—anything—when things are not working, rather than worrying about doing the right thing.

"Back when I first took over the area, I thought after the first month that I had been assigned to adult day care. It wasn't just that the results were off. They were, but you could not find anyone who would own up to things being the way they were, and they were pathetic. The previous manager had been here a long, long time; she had just over 30 years with the company when she retired, and she had been in the position for 12 years. When she took over, the department had only been going for about two years, so she was responsible for inventing a lot of the way things were done.

"You know as well as I do that this company has been built on its sales organization. A lot of times, the sales folks can seem aggressive to the rest of us. For this lady, it was just not in her deck to ever play the confrontation card, so anytime there was any hint of controversy she encouraged her group to accommodate. Unfortunately, over time, the practices here became very localized and convoluted. It was almost like they spoke their own language but, as long as the sales rolled in, their sins were covered up. Four years ago, the economy slowed. So did our sales, and that's when the chickens came home to roost. What was discovered as we attempted to squeeze our profitability from operating efficiencies is that this group's practices were so parochial that the department literally didn't mesh with those around it. It became a bottleneck as attempts were made to streamline the process. Like I said, that was about four years ago. The heat got turned up, and my predecessor took the opportunity to leave rather than make the changes that were needed. I was asked to take this area on. I did so willingly, but without a lot of due diligence. I think if I had done my homework, I still would have accepted the position, but would have had a better idea what I was getting into."

At this point, Carolyn chimes in with a question. "Well, what about the previous two attempts though? Why didn't this approach click right from the start?"

"Thanks for asking, Carolyn, I am getting to that and I probably should speed up a bit in the interest of time. But I think it is important for you to know that the turnaround in this area, and there has been one, was not an overnight sensation and certainly was not because I rode in on my charger and slew some dragon that had perpetually tortured the village. In my view, what happened here could have happened anyplace. Anyplace that relies too much on the judgment or guidance of one person, and doesn't expect well-paid and bright managers to make decisions and clean up their own messes. Like I said, I thought I had been assigned to adult day care.

"When I arrived, the guiding principle was 'do whatever you need to do to keep our customers happy.' For these folks, a customer meant anyone outside the area, so everyone was a customer and everyone was treated that way to a fault. When I arrived, almost no one was getting what they wanted from us because everything we did was a one-off and there was no way to determine from one situation to the next what would be done. It seemed to depend entirely on each of my local managers' mood at the moment.

"My first attempt to make some immediate changes was to insist that all the managers in my area work together to make process decisions. Some of the folks you saw in the session yesterday were a part of the group, but not everyone. Since they were used to making the customer happy and I was the newest customer, they all said yes and started meeting once a month for about two hours. Nothing changed! What I discovered after a short while was that they spent most of their time commiserating about how difficult the customers were. So, after about three months of meetings in this format, I shut the group down. By the way, there were no complaints.

"I talked with a couple of my managers who I had developed some trust in, and asked for their analysis. The input they gave me should have been obvious in the first place, but it wasn't. In their view, putting people together who had their decisions made for them for years, then asking them to make decisions, was just too much to expect. These were bright enough people, but you know how it is in organizations—no matter what decision you make, somebody is not going to like it, and these folks were not prepared for dealing with any pushback as part of the process. Pushback meant they did something wrong, and in all of their discussions, they reached a point where they would anticipate pushback and immediately abandon the idea."

I have been listening to what Bev is saying, and now realize that the group I had been transferred to lead had initially suffered some of the very same symptoms. The manager who preceded me had been a good guy, but, as with many areas at MoneyPump, ours had grown quickly and he had probably taken too much of the decision-making onto himself. A great approach when you want something fast, but not necessarily when you want something everyone will own or that will be sustainable when you are not around.

"Bev, I know that making people's decisions for them is not your style. Were you ever tempted to do that when this first attempt stalled out?"

"Another great question, Ron...and no, I wasn't. But my manager was; he wanted results fast and he made that very clear to me. He and I had more than one heated conversation—he more heated than me, of course. I always stay cool!" Bev smiles her special killer smile at this. "He was all for simply telling people what to do and getting on with it. My response to him was that it wasn't that simple. Certainly, my folks needed to step up and begin to make decisions, but the groups they had interacted with, provided services to, and were co-conspirators in the bottlenecking process needed to step up as well. My manager agreed with me in principle on that notion, but wanted to know how I was going to deal with it.

"I suggested a return to the peer group sessions that I had started with. He immediately pushed back on that idea, saying that it hadn't worked and he couldn't see the sense in going back to the same approach. I explained to him that the difference this time would be twofold. First, I would make participation from my group voluntary. It hadn't occurred to me the first time that my managers never gave a thought to saying no to my idea; they were just used to going along with everything. Second, I would enlist the support of a couple of directors at my level from our customer groups and see if we could invite some of their managers to join us. He asked me how I knew this would work, and I said I didn't. The logic I finally used to get my manager's support was that, if we knew what to do, we'd have already been doing it. So obviously, we didn't know what to do; the way to learn was to begin making changes. He needed to give me some cover to make a few mistakes, but he knew my track record.

"I knew playing the old 'track record' card was good for at least one more chance, and he gave it to me. It took several conversations with the directors at my level, but they were just unhappy enough to try my plan. It took a couple more conversations with folks we wanted in, but eventually they saw the logic, or at least admitted that they had nothing to lose, and decided to join in. One specific difference this time was that I wanted to keep a short leash on the group, and insisted that at the first sign of stalling out they get me back involved. After two months, they came to me; one of my managers and one from an outside group. They wanted my help. They had seen that there was a possibility of something valuable taking place, but they realized quickly that they had no talent for consensus. Conversations that started with lots of promise got bogged down whenever any signs of strong differences of opinion or emotions showed up. My guys just went turtle, and the dialogue quickly became a monologue. They suggested that there be a facilitator for the group and they thought I would be perfect."

Sheryl speaks now for the first time since we started. "So, did you agree? I mean, was Sonja just filling in yesterday while you met with Ron and Carolyn?"

"Actually, I think you'll be very interested in the answer to your question, Sheryl, but I need a short break. Maybe 15 minutes, does that work for everyone?"

—

So, Bev is not a sorceress after all; her success is built on the learning that had occurred from a couple of failed attempts to realize her desired outcome. For me, this is good news. I consider Bev to be a master manager. If someone with her skill set had taken her lumps trying to get something new to work, then there is hope for me as well. Her "story" of success following failure will be a key to selling the idea of initiating this approach over in my area, and I imagined that Carolyn and Sheryl will have some selling to do as well. One thing about working in successful organizations is that they develop a high degree of immunity to change. They can also be hesitant to associate with failure. I arrived after much of our initial success had been achieved, so I have been cautioned by more than one superior about not taking unnecessary risks. One of the things that you don't realize until you work for a very successful company is just how much gets swept under the rug because the company can afford not to deal with it. Personally, I am thanking my lucky stars that Carolyn arrived at my office door yesterday morning. Whether she realizes it or not, her intolerance for the mediocre is going to end up making a difference in a lot of people's performance before we are done.

But back to the moment at hand. Bev's answer to Sheryl's question is going to let us know whether she had really created something new here, or if she had merely re-invented micromanagement. I think I know what her answer will be, but can't wait to hear the story behind it.

# CHAPTER 14

# SHE MAY NOT BE A SORCERESS BUT SHE IS ONE SMART COOKIE!

While Bev and Marty are taking their break, Carolyn, Sheryl, and I stay in the room to debrief a bit on what we have heard so far. We all agree that it is comforting to find that Bev is human after all, and had failed a couple of times to get where she wanted to go. But we are also experienced enough as managers to know that you can make something look better than it really is, as long as you get results. You can take a highly directive approach to managing and expect a lot of slack from senior managers who don't want to mess with a good thing. The next few minutes will tell us whether we have a future applying what Bev developed in our own groups. We are all very committed to a facilitative style of managing as much as possible, and hope what we are going to hear will be aligned with that approach.

—

Bev and Marty rejoin us, and Bev jumps right back in where we had left off. "Did I become their group facilitator? Oh, no. When they asked me to facilitate, I had two things to say: One, an outside facilitator seemed like a great idea, and two, having me in there would defeat my intention of these folks discovering how to reach decisions at a peer level. They were so steeped in having decisions made for them that they would acquiesce if I gave them any hint of a preference, and they would likely infer one if I didn't."

"So, how did Sonja end up in there?" Sheryl asks. "She doesn't normally spend time away from the classroom setting."

Bev grins again. "She interviewed for the job and they hired her. Well, in a manner of speaking. They asked her to join them as their facilitator."

This sounds a bit too easy for me, and Bev picks up on my body language. "Okay, Ron, it wasn't that simple, but here's how Sonja got the invitation. At my suggestion, the two managers who had initially come to me invited Sonja to get together. They met, they explained what they were looking for, and then they talked for a while about their expectations. Then Sonja did something they didn't expect. She told them she was interested, but not if they were going to continue with the format they had been using. She explained to them that she would only accept the role if they would agree to lengthen their sessions to three hours and add in an extra two hours every two weeks for additional work on their own. Her experience led her to conclude that this was a group that needed to engage in some professional development along with the addition of a facilitator."

Bev is shifting into fast forward mode in the interest of time, but I don't want to rush. My preference would be to move slower and, if possible, not repeat Bev's missteps if we decide to go down this path. "Bev, did you know she was going to do that? Add in the requirement for the extra hour?"

"Oh, yes. Sonja has known me for a while but didn't want to just assume I would concur with the change to the format, so we talked about it before she sprung it on my gang. When she brought it up, it immediately made sense for a couple of reasons. First, while my managers had all participated in the management development curriculum offered here at MoneyPump, Sonja was quick to point out the shortcomings of the approach of the company, and she is one of the lead instructors!

"Managers need knowledge in two specific areas where our programs are weak. One is self-knowledge. Most of our managers were originally strong individual contributors who moved up to supervisors, and then into the roles they now play. What they learned in our programs was valuable, but primarily technique and situational; a lot of what not to do if you recall your own sessions. Sonja had been looking for an opportunity to provide our managers with deeper understanding of themselves as people and how they affect those around them. In her mind, this program could be that opportunity; provided, of course, that the managers would agree to extend the sessions. She did have some selling to do there. Around MoneyPump, 'soft stuff' tends to be a hard sell.

"The second area of weakness our programs have, in Sonja's mind, is that there is a built-in assumption that, because the company appoints you as a manager, everybody else will accept you as one—meaning the people who report to you, your peers, and so on. Sonja thinks this assumption is based on outdated ideas. Four generations of managers have moved through the workplace since many of our management ideas were first formulated. Three of these generations are in the workplace now, and there are significant differences among them. What managers must understand now is that being appointed by the company confers on you the responsibility to develop extraordinary working CONNECTIONS, where something more casual may have been acceptable in your other roles here. If you look—and I did, after Sonja talked about this—our programs at all levels assume that managers are given the authority to get the job done and need to figure out how to use it. We do not stress or teach managers how to build the CONNECTIONS they need."

Sheryl is deep in thought, having just heard what Bev had to say. Carolyn is looking right at me and asks, "Do you agree with that, Ron?"

After a slight hesitation, I said, "I hadn't really thought about it before this moment, but what Bev just said makes me think that one of the differences between me and some others, who I know are very bright but haven't moved up, is that I am just naturally good at building the CONNECTIONS I need with my reports and peers.

Bev is pointing out a really important distinction to us, and, while I hadn't given it a lot of thought, intuitively I agree with what she is saying."

At this moment, Sheryl comes back from her deep reflection. "I can't tell you the number of times I have seen a manager struggle and wondered why they don't just go talk to whoever, or see that they need to talk with so-and-so about it. It has never occurred to me that they don't know what to do or how to have the conversation. I feel like slapping my forehead and shouting, 'Duh!'"

Bev comes back in at this point. "Well, Sheryl, if you should be slapping your forehead, a lot of us would be joining you, including me. CONNECTION building is so natural for me at this point in my career that I guess I had just assumed when it wasn't there for other people, it was a choice they were making. That's why the conversation Sonja had with me was so enlightening, and why I immediately agreed to support her idea for the additional time."

"It sounds to me," says Sheryl, "like MoneyPump should be redesigning the management development series we all went through. Is Sonja saying that the management development sessions we've been doing are not worthwhile? I am sure that would not be a popular point of view among her colleagues."

"No, quite the opposite, she thinks the sessions are valuable; they just are not sufficient. Her metaphor is that our senior leadership approaches the development process like it's a car wash...where your car is supposed to stay permanently clean once it goes through. That may seem silly at first, but think about how many times a senior manager has said something to the effect of, 'I thought these people were already trained.'

"MoneyPump requires all managers to participate in a series of development sessions held at the central training center. This is a fairly typical approach, I guess. I know you both went through the programs so you know what I am about to say. The programs last nearly a week each, they are spaced about a year apart, and you attend with people who are not part of your work group who you may never see again. After each one, you head back to your work group and no one talks to you about what you learned or how you are going to apply the knowledge. When you complete the third session, that's it; you're done developing. Some of it sticks, most of it doesn't, but all the appropriate boxes get checked. Don't get me wrong, I am not inferring that we shouldn't be doing our management development this way. Sonja's point was that something more was needed to leverage the investment the company had been making, and this solution seemed to her like maybe it would provide the framework that would bring everything together. She kept referring to it as 'bringing a process approach to development.' She also likened it to a fitness regimen. I don't have a fitness regimen, so I had to take her word for that."

Sheryl looks perplexed at this last statement, and words just come popping out of her mouth. "So, you are actually repeating material that's been covered in the other three sessions. Has anybody complained about that?"

"Sheryl, you are not the first person who has asked that question. When I told my manager what we were going to do, he said the same thing. 'Why are you going to repeat what they have already learned?' was his way of putting it. If we had arrived at today's meeting earlier, you would have seen the material Sonja was presenting. It may or may not have looked familiar. For the most part, the folks in the group have had vague recollections of most of the material and have been glad for the opportunity to go over it again with people they work with regularly. It is not a heavy dose of material, maybe an hour-and-a-half at each session, but it builds on previous sessions. They have homework, not much, just enough so they need to apply what they were exposed to. 'Exposed' is Sonja's term. She says that the Management Development sessions we do are really 'exposure' sessions. We expose our managers to many new ideas and methods for managing, and then expect them to handle the application on their own. The truth is that, in the sessions, they really learn very little, if by learn we mean retain and apply as needed. What we are doing in the peer group is bringing back material they have been exposed to in a context where it can be applied immediately and then reinforced through the group process. She is completely thrilled by what has been happening because she feels like there is finally an opportunity for the learning she has always intended to be completed."

"Unfortunately, this reminded me of the conversation I had with my manager last spring when I was suggesting an expense for refresher courses in handling conflict for my managers. That request didn't get approved. Ouch!"

Carolyn starts gathering up her things. "So, that's it then?" I can tell she is eager to move ahead. "It took you three tries to get to this point and now you think you've got it, right? I am glad we took this time, Bev, and I guess the next step is to talk with Sonja and see about using her to facilitate similar groups for us. I know you have moved things around to make the time for us, but it seems like we should let you get back to what you were doing before we interrupted you." This is typical Carolyn; she wants to get into action and solve the problem.

Bev is now smiling in a way that lets me know Carolyn has just fallen into another of her little traps. "I am guessing that you think I had something better to do than spend this time with you. Actually, tomorrow Marty and I are hosting another very similar meeting for a group of directors from our marketing department. We have two similar meetings next week for two other sections."

Carolyn's face reddens a bit. "But I thought you were a director and had your own results to produce?"

"Well I am and I do…but you've met Marty. He's a very capable guy and a quick study. Fortunately, he came to me right as this process was beginning to get legs and requests started to come in from other business units to come around and see what was working so well here. He is still manager-in-training, but he's sort of de facto become director-in-training. Actually, more like director. In fact, over the past three months, we have been swamped with requests. I am spending more and more of my time with other directors bringing them the 'good word,' if you will. It is a dream come true for me."

"You might be surprised to hear this, but I have been shocked at how quickly this idea has gained popularity. There was a time when many people were threatened by the success of others, and made up stories about how they got lucky or something like that; very competitive reactions. What seems to be happening now is that the complexity of our offerings, technology, and the changes in our work force are doing that 'perfect storm' thing that seems to be so popular to talk about. I don't know if it is perfect, but it sure is stormy for a lot of managers these days. They are looking for help now, anywhere they can find it. Timing is everything!"

Carolyn continues her gathering process, "Well, I am glad to know we'll be in good company then, and no doubt Sonja won't be surprised to hear from us."

Now Bev stands and goes to the conference room door. "If it is Sonja you want, stick around." She opens the door. "Sonja, they are all yours now…if they decide to stay."

Sonja bounces into the room with a "Ta da! I brought cookies!"

# CHAPTER 15
# SONJA...AND WHAT SHE WANTS TO TELL US

Sonja quickly gathered us around the conference room table. "I did bring cookies, but since I know you all have time constraints, I don't think we should take a break. Let's just pass the cookies and dive right in. What questions do you have?"

Okay, so right from the start Sonja is scoring points. Carolyn, Sheryl, and myself are all results-oriented managers, and her action-focused approach is going to win us over right away.

As usual, Carolyn is ready with a question. "How do we get started?" she blurts out. Sonja isn't just action-oriented, she is also cool under fire.

"Well, that might seem to be the question, but let me stage it based on my experience. The critical question will eventually be how to get started, but, before that, there is an even more important question: Where to get started? I don't know if you thought about this but, without sufficient motive, there is no reason for any of the people you just saw working to be in the room. They don't have to be there; it is their choice to be there. They are there because it is in their interest to be there."

My curiosity gets the best of me. "What do you mean by motive and self-interest?"

At that, Sonja smiles. "Listen, all of you have been managers for a while. Well, I have been involved in management development for probably as long as you've each been managing. One thing we all know for sure is that there is a big difference working with people, whether they report to us or show up in our classrooms, who are motivated either to succeed or learn. Sometimes those two things are one and the same. I can tell you from experience that working with these learning communities is nothing like being in the classroom. In the classroom, I was always directing the agenda. People had little at stake, save for the time they were spending in the classroom. Sure, sometimes I got a higher percentage of people in who were interested in learning the art and science of management, but, more often than not, they wanted to be able to check the box that said they had completed Management Level 2 or whatever was next on their annual development plan. I know this sounds harsh but, over the years, I sort of resigned myself to delivering good programs and hoping that some of what we offered would stick. This, by the way, is not just my experience; there are lots of research results that back me up. But, we persisted in this approach because we were locked into an educational design that convinced us we needed to be running in-house schools or universities. Development and classrooms were sort of joined at the hip. It wasn't until I got involved with Bev's groups that the lightbulb went off. See, I had been reading about a 70–20–10 learning theory for a while.[6] And before you ask, 70 + 20 + 10 obviously equals 100. In this case, the 10 stands for 10 percent and refers to a formula that makes up a learning experience based on 10 percent formal or classroom coursework or training.

The 20 percent refers to developmental CONNECTIONS, or communities of practice, or networking, mentoring, and of course the manager/superior CONNECTION."

"And what about the 70 percent?" I ask, to show just how well I am paying attention.

"Hold your ponies, Mr. Wallace," Sonja responds. "I'll get there. People in my profession have been faced with pressure from line managers to cut down the time in the classroom for years. So, we've seen increased reliance on self-directed learning, lots of money being spent on eLearning modules, webinars, virtual classroom events, and the like. All very high-tech of course, and presumably less time-consuming than the previous strictly-classroom-based models. But ultimately, except for less time in the classroom, this approach has proven to be no more effective than the previous model."

Sheryl jumps in at this point. "But what about mentoring? Surely that has had a positive impact?" At this Sonja again smiles, but not a happy smile; more like a "I'm sorry I have to tell you this" smile.

"Mentoring, as it turns out, does not lend itself very well to a program approach. People, of course, have good intentions and want to be team players, but then something with an apparently higher priority comes up and poof—there goes the mentoring. The manager/superior CONNECTION remains the most reliable source of this type of development but, again, this does not lend itself to a programmatic approach. Time-stressed managers will find ways to circumvent the program requirements. Their superiors often default to narratives that claim necessity when pushed to get involved.

Here's the truth: If you get a manager highly committed to your development, good for you. If not…"

I can't stand it; I just have to ask. "But what we just saw was obviously working; wasn't that a community of practice?"

"Have a cookie, Ron, you are getting warmer!" With that, Sonja passes her basket and continues. "What you just sat in on was a meeting of a 'Community of Mutual Success.' Now, give me a little slack here. I am a professional and we always must have our own vocabulary to distinguish our profession. 'Community of Mutual Success' is the name I gave to what otherwise would have been called, 'one of Bev's groups.' Remember when I said there was a 70 percent component, but then didn't discuss it?" We all nodded. "That 70 percent number in the development literature refers to 'Challenging Assignments.' If you were ever part of an accelerated manager's development program, you might recall being moved around periodically through various positions, or challenging assignments, with the intention of rapidly moving you to higher levels of responsibility.

"These programs had pretty good track records, but in all honesty, not because the programs were successful but because of the selection criteria—kind of like prestigious universities are very good at selecting incoming freshmen they already know have a high likelihood of doing well in their environment; a self-fulfilling prophecy, if you will.

"What I saw when I began to work with Bev's groups was that there was a diverse mix of management talent in each group, but the way Bev, crafty Bev, had put the groups together, the one thing they had in common was that everyone in the room was in some way dependent on at least one other person there—who they had no authority over—for their success. Learning to work at increasingly higher levels of productivity with their dependent connection was going to be these folks 70 percent, their Challenging Assignment. And these groups were not made up of senior managers-in-waiting; they were career mid-level managers, like most managers are.

"Remember earlier when I said it mattered that people in the group have motive and some sense of self interest? There it is, right in the design. These groups are convened by invitation only, no one is required to attend, and a manager cannot attend just any old group. They can attend and become part of a group they have been invited to."

Sheryl is quick to ask, "Who decides on the invitation list?"

"Another good question," acknowledges Sonja. "Initially, Bev created the invitation lists. It was a bit tricky since she planned to invite managers who did not report to her. She had to do some groundwork with managers in other functional areas. Not all of them were quickly sold on the concept, but Bev was relentless in pitching the self-interest aspect of the groups and the voluntary participation. The groups were formed up around projects in some cases, but what Bev primarily had in mind was groups formed cross-functionally involving an ongoing process that led to customer satisfaction. What has been an interesting value to the groups is the amount of education that has gone on: Managers are well versed in their functional areas operationally, but not so much across functional lines. I don't know if compassion is a good word to use, but certainly respect has been elevated as the various managers come to understand the challenges their cross-functional counterparts face."

"And you say results have improved?" pipes in Carolyn, with her ever-bottom-line outlook.

"Without question. And in a range of measurable areas," chirps Sonja. "Almost always, a group was formed because there was a lag or drag in some customer serving functional chain. In some cases, the lag was identified internally as opportunity, and in others, customers pointed out the need for improvement. It didn't matter in the end; improvement was the objective and all sources were considered valid."

Sheryl jumps back in quickly, "You mentioned a range of measurable improvement. Can you give us examples?"

"Some of the results have been surprising!" Sonja informs us happily. "There were, of course, primary goals which involved process and quality improvements. What came about as side effects included reduced turnover and improvements in engagement scores. Of course, these were indirect results, kind of unintended good consequences, if you will, but there does seem to be some corollary impact on these measures where the 'Communities of Mutual Success' have been in place for a while. The groups primary goals are usually satisfied sooner rather than later, in most cases, and then the corollary results follow in time."

"Sonja, I am sure you get this question from time to time. You mentioned that some groups have been operating for quite a while, I am guessing beyond the satisfaction of the goals for which they were originally established. What keeps them together?" I ask this with genuine curiosity, as I know these managers are under demands like my own in terms of time. Yet, I didn't see anyone looking at watches or cell phones during the session we sat in on.

"Ron, now you are getting to the real value. It was more discovered than intended. Imagine yourself sitting in a room of people who are openly committed to your success here at MoneyPump. Then, imagine that, in turn, you are as committed to their success—each and every one there. Imagine also that, in this group, you could talk about anything that affected your work, including personal stuff at home, knowing that, no matter what was discussed, you could expect the details to stay contained within the group. How valuable would that be to you? And how much attention do you think you'd put on those three hours a month in terms of making sure you were there?"

Sonja's question stops me briefly. "So, you're telling me that was why everyone was paying such close attention in that session?"

"Well, I can't speak for everyone there, but the short answer is yes." Sonja smiles her warmest smile yet.

Carolyn, likely the least warm and fuzzy of the three of us, quickly joins in. "So then, Sonja, how did you get involved and what is your commitment?" Back to the bottom line!

"Yes, that is a good question. I was invited to, and I sort of auditioned for the role I play in there. This group came to a point shortly after it was formed when the members realized they would benefit from the support of an un-invested facilitator. They couldn't very well ask their managers; that would diminish the safety in the minds of some. After some discussion, they decided that since there was a previous CONNECTION with some of them from the management development sessions, they would approach me to see if I might be interested. All it took for me was a description of what they were looking for, and I was hooked. Once I met the group and got a sense of what they were committed to, I quickly went from excited to anxious, hoping I'd pass the interview or whatever criteria they set up to make a choice. The way this was described was a management developers dream come true. Voluntary participation, safe space for discussion, seeing management excellence as requiring an ongoing practice. Oh, and did I fail to mention focus on talent development?

"Then there was one more thing, and this was the clincher for me: These folks were mid-level managers who knew they were mid-level managers and they were looking to get better at their craft."

Carolyn, with her usual impatience, pops into Sonja's explanation. "I don't get it. These people were settling for being mid-level managers; they didn't have any higher expectations?"

"Spoken like someone on their way up the career ladder," says Sonja. "You are speaking from your own frame of reference, Carolyn, as a senior manager in waiting, and it's not just you, but anyone who works with you, who knows you are on your way up. No, these people were plenty ambitious but, as they had worked together and gotten to know each other, they began to realize that their skills, talents, and interests were best suited to managing in the middle. They had, in fact, found their calling, and now their objective was mastery. Where they excelled was in translating senior management objectives and strategy into action and outcomes for the corporation and, after a few sessions together, they had one thing in common. They knew they were where they belonged, and that their greatest contribution was the identification and development of future talent for the corporation. They were in the best position day to day to observe performance and identify people that had more to offer than was being asked of them."

Carolyn looks a bit taken aback, but recovers quickly. "I get it now; you're right, I was looking at this from my point of view and through my ambitions. But when I think about it, in my desire to reach a senior position, I also know that these are the types of people I'll be counting on to keep the talent flowing through our workplace."

With that, we turn our attention to the mechanics and details of how we can get "Communities of Mutual Success" going in our own areas. Sonja made it very clear that she is now partnered with Bev, and they both had created a CONNECTION with the head of management development and his boss, the head of talent for the corporation. MoneyPump is ahead of a lot of companies I am aware of, in that the company has reassigned many traditional Human Resource functions to areas where it makes more sense. Payroll went to Finance; Benefits went to Risk Management; and Human Resources became intently focused on talent acquisition, development, and retention. That became their sole purpose for existing; in fact, so much so that the functional area was renamed Talent and the term Human Resources simply disappeared. Nobody seems to miss it, either.

I mention this partnership between Bev and the folks in Talent because their approach is unique, and it took a leap of faith to proceed as they did. Despite their positive experiences with the "Communities of Mutual Success," there is not going to be any corporate-wide CMS initiative or campaign. Bev, Sonja, and her managers are convinced that attraction, rather than promotion, is a key determinant of the success of the groups this far. Make it corporate, give it goals, and, in no time, participation would no longer be voluntary. The spirit, spontaneity, and organic nature would be squeezed out. Going through the motions would replace the vitality we saw in the group we sat with. Nope, if we are going to get involved, it needs to be on our own initiative. Bev will counsel, of course. Sonja will consult, but we will bear the burden of attracting and developing our own "Communities of Success." As this message sinks in, I ask my associates, "So?"

They both respond quickly, "We're in!" And so, our journey begins...

# CHAPTER 16
# FAST FORWARD, SO HOW DID OUR COOKIES TURN OUT?

Nine months have passed since that meeting with Sonja. It wasn't our last meeting with her, and from time to time we still check in. Sonja continues to serve as facilitator for the group we sat with back when we knew nothing about Communities of Mutual Success (CMS). In addition to that, she has taken on another role as developmental mentor to other facilitators of similar groups. I wouldn't say that CMS's have become a movement at MoneyPump, but there are now 15 groups in one stage or another of development, and interest has been expressed elsewhere. Most of the senior management members are aware that the CMS process has begun and is gaining popularity. Wisely, they are treating CMS as an emergent process and allowing it to grow on its own merits. As a company, MoneyPump was already doing well, and the benefits of the CMS groups are being treated like found money. No one has expressed any intent or interest in attempting to manage CMS like a program, and we are all grateful for that. Our experience has taught us that the power of the CMS groups comes from their voluntary, organic nature. Since members of these groups are operating primarily from a discretionary posture, we are beginning to see just how much energy can be harnessed by tapping the lateral capacity that is revealed when self-interest can be unleashed in a healthy way.

Now, don't think that our process has been a bed of roses. All three of us—Carolyn, Sheryl, and myself—set out to establish a CMS in our area. Given our varying personalities, each of us took a somewhat different path to getting our groups up and running. Carolyn, our driver and result producer, initially could not overcome her controlling nature and quickly created her group, enrolled her lateral managers, and put her team in place. The obvious problem, of course, was that everything was her idea and nobody showed up owning anything. Members attended the meetings because nobody wanted to get crosswise with Carolyn. After about four months, the group ground to a halt when five of the nine members called the day of their session claiming a need to be elsewhere. Carolyn was disappointed, but she is also a fast learner. She is now three months into a restart with a much more voluntary and organic feel. The group has gained some traction and, though progress is not as quick as Carolyn would prefer, she is pacing herself with lots of deep breathing and time spent on other projects.

Sheryl, on the other hand, ran into different kinds of issues. She is one to suggest things to her managers and hope they pick up the thread of the opportunity. She received some sparks of interest, mainly from individual managers taking the initiative to cross functional lines; but no group formed, and she has now called on Sonja to coach her in getting the message across to her managers.

My experience has been quite different, largely, I think, because I took a more methodical approach. But then, that's me—methodical to the bitter end.

So, let me tell you about my initial foray into CMS sponsorship.

I started by talking with the managers who reported to me. The initial discussion centered around where we were disappointed with the service we were providing to the end customer. Once we identified areas of our own dissatisfaction, I asked what, if anything, we could do to improve the service. The answers that came back were varied, but to summarize, my managers came to the conclusion I expected: There were things we could do, but only so much since there were other functions involved in providing the service as it finally appeared to the customer.

Then, I asked whether we had done anything to engage the other functional areas in our interest to improve the level of service we were providing. As I expected, the answer was yes. While a similar level of commitment was expressed by our colleagues in the participating functions, the results over time had been less than spectacular. When I asked my managers for their view on why their commitment and the commitment of their counterparts in the other functions were not what was hoped for, their responses ranged from personality assessments to competing priorities to competency critiques and much more. In the end, there was no single view that prevailed, and together we concluded that we truly did not know why we continued to provide less than the service we were committed to.

As you are reading this, you may begin to lose patience with the pace I am reporting. Just know that I fully anticipated that, and want to take a moment to point out that the impatience you are experiencing is the biggest threat to any CMS process being successful.

Remember Bev's drawing from earlier in our story...

## Theory of Outcomes in Organizations

Outcomes
Action
Opportunity
Possibility
Inherited Connection

While it may not be immediately apparent, what I was doing at this point with my managers was laying the foundation and identifying CONNECTIONS. I walked them into a realization that their CONNECTIONS with their counterparts might not be set up for them to succeed.

During these discussions, it became apparent that my managers were relying on a strategy of everyone doing their part. Since their counterparts knew their functional areas best, they would decide on the actions that would realize the improvements. My managers reported that, in some cases, the actions promised by their counterparts were completed without appreciable service improvement; and, in others, they found that the actions promised got subordinated by demands from their higher-ups.

When I finally asked my managers if they felt they were set up to succeed in their collaborative efforts, they sheepishly admitted that they felt constrained, and were embarrassed that they had not seen this fact for themselves. I quickly assured them that no blame was intended; the discussion I engaged with them was exactly like the one I thought they needed to have with their counterparts. I went on to ask if they were interested in possibly altering the CONNECTIONS with their counterparts, and each of them said yes despite have some skepticism.

Once we passed through this gateway—them acknowledging both their interest and willingness to pursue the service improvement—I gave them some idea of how a CMS worked, and what I had seen with my own eyes. I cannot say that they jumped for joy at what I described, but they did admit that the time involved was not too demanding and that the time they were currently spending was not producing the result. So, why not give it a try?

That admission was all I needed to get rolling. From this conversation, I proceeded to meet with my counterparts in the service delivery process and shared my vision of what was possible. Again, there was some expression of skepticism, but also an acknowledgement of a shared sense of frustration at our seeming inability to affect our service levels despite repeated attempts with some pretty capable people.

And so we began...

In my mind, while my approach is methodical, my commitment is fierce, and I saw this project as laying the foundation for an entirely new way of doing day-to-day business, not only for my area, but for MoneyPump. So, I wasn't going to take any chances. I pitched Sonja hard, and she accepted my request to be directly involved. She did have some stipulations.

Sonja insisted on taking the learning from the other CMS's and bringing that to my group early on so they did not need to reinvent methods that had been proven successful in other groups. That request received my full approval, provided that Sonja presented those ideas as options and not direct instructions. She agreed.

Since I was the primary sponsor of the CMS approach, my counterparts asked me to hold conversations with their reports as well. As with my reports, the light went on slowly, but eventually it began to shine brightly and people committed to participate.

With Sonja, I agreed that we would not give the CMS project a big "launch." All these managers had seen the big project launch in the past. In their minds, it signified something we did not want to promote—the idea that a CMS was like a project and it had a beginning, middle, and an end. We wanted the participating managers to discover the "practice" nature of the CMS themselves, and we also wanted the continuation of the group, following initial successes, to be their idea.

Back to Sonja's stipulations. One of the primary discoveries that Sonja had made with her other CMS groups was that everyone participating had many competing commitments and centers of gravity that influenced their actions. Unless there were some principles put in place—even simple guidelines—the boundaries of the CMS would be hard to hold, and the practice would be attacked by outside forces and eventually defeated. These attacks would not be malicious; they would be simply be environmental factors to be accounted for in order to sustain the CMS identity.

At the very first gathering of our CMS, Sonja suggested to the group that they adopt the following guidelines developed by earlier CMS groups, with the understanding that they would take a while to appreciate fully. Here's what she showed them:

## GUIDELINES FOR SUSTAINING A CMS
**Using Enlightened Self-Interest to Stay Sane, Productive, and Amused as We Work Together**

1. Show up—attendance is critical. Group performance depends on participation.

2. Whoever sees it first gets to do it.

3. Nobody likes anybody's ideas better than their own. Everyone wants to play; they will play your game if they can play their way—let them.

4. Organizational life will provide as much nonsense as you can deal with; do not contribute to the chaos.

5. Do not confuse your beliefs with the truth; it makes you stupid and an annoyance to other people.

6. Where you have no control, you must communicate. When you do not communicate, apologize. When someone fails to communicate with you, forgive.

7. If you only need to share information, email is great. If you need to communicate, pick up the phone or walk down the hall. Communication is a process inside a relationship inside a context, not a transaction.

8. Give up your right to say, "I told you so!" If you don't say it when you first see it, forget it and get to work.

9. We are all, as individuals, in over our heads. That's just the way it is.

10. Keep your expectations consistent with only what has been promised. Anything else you get is a bonus, and you have no basis for ever expecting to get it again.

11. Limit your opinions to only those things to which you are truly committed and prepared to take action on.

12. Toughen up. Life is a contact sport anyway; organizational life is worse!

13. Get curious—stay curious.

14. Give your gifts willingly.

15. Remember...if you can't laugh at yourself, someone else will always be happy to do it for you.

A full understanding of the value of these guidelines would likely take months to achieve, but the group was sufficiently committed to the objective of service improvement that they were willing to surrender the need to understand in the interest of the overall objective. (See Appendix A)

You might imagine, since I am now reporting to you from nine months into the process, that everything went smoothly. You would be very wrong. We started slowly and are still on our initial set of objectives, but—before you ask what's wrong—consider this. The level of service we previously provided was not pathetic; it just wasn't what we knew we needed for a competitive advantage. There was no barn burning that need attention.

In addition, the process improvement we sought was one element of a very complex CONNECTION with our customers that, while important, was by no means the only place our energies were directed. If we didn't take things slowly, we'd 1) create a project mindset and 2) create prioritization where it was not necessary. The value, as I saw it, was in the long term. While improving the service level was important, it was nowhere near as valuable as the capacity we were building through the CMS approach.

The members of my CMS are now themselves reporting that they realize the CMS is an emergent practice. In private conversations, they have observed that the likelihood of achieving our initial objectives is quite high—almost a certainty, given more time and working together. More importantly, from their perspective, they are recognizing a new depth in their working CONNECTIONS, both with their departmental colleagues and their cross-functional counterparts. As we move forward, they are seeing the opportunities to address issues begin to emerge as if a fog is being lifted. Well, that's sort of dramatic, but one of the managers did say that!

I have long believed that, as an organization, we were viewed by the customer as a single entity; but we operated in loose alliances of fiefdoms and did not have the same view of ourselves as the customer. Unfortunately, much of the way we managed, evaluated, and rewarded our employees didn't do much to encourage the customer view. We treated everyone individually, then expected unbridled collaboration. Not very smart, and we are still working on it.

But, I digress—you know this from your own experience.

As our newly formed CMS took shape and began to address the service levels, Sonja discovered that our managers, when put together with their colleagues in a situation where there were high stakes, all acted very guarded. Sonja had advised me to expect this, so as the guardedness surfaced, it was dealt with. This was new for everyone. Historically, guardedness was simply tolerated and worked over the top of. With Sonja's help, the member managers began to realize that they could deal with the guardedness and, in fact, replace it with an atmosphere of safety.

She suggested some ground rules that other groups had adopted to create a safe environment. Now, if you are just trying to produce a result against some timeline, a typical project approach, you still should focus on creating an environment of safety. The difference with a CMS is that you use the result to be produced as an excuse to build the capacity of the group.

As you can probably see from my description of our experience, we are a long way from where we were that day Carolyn showed up in my doorway looking for advice. At the same time, we are a long way from finished. In fact, we've stopped worrying about finishing and recognize that there is no finish line to be concerned about. There is only the CMS process and the challenges it allows us to face as we get better together.

Are there still questions to work out the answers for? You bet. What about Sheryl? What if she doesn't get her CMS off the ground? Will that kill support for other managers going forward? What about Carolyn? Being a rising star, she is likely to get promoted soon; who will sponsor her CMS then? What about this notion of management practice? Does it replace project management?

It used to be that our organization and I needed have the answers to questions like these before we committed to action or got sponsorship. Now we see that as an old way of doing business. The world we live in no longer waits for certainty. Ambiguity abounds, and what was okay yesterday doesn't cut it today. What matters is the capacity to respond. That's what the CMS practice is doing for us; building capacity in the same way that getting out and exercising first builds and then maintains fitness.

Check back with us in another nine months. My instincts say that my CMS group will still be going and be even stronger. As for Sheryl and Carolyn, time will tell, but judging a practice like CMS on a one-by-one basis is likely not the way to determine overall value.

# CHAPTER 17
# SOME PARTING THOUGHTS

Okay, that's the last we are going to hear from Ron, Carolyn, Sheryl, Bev, Marty, and Sonja. As you have been reading, you may have been reflecting on your own organization and developmental experiences. Don't be too hard on either yourself or your organization. The global economy has revealed that many of us were not quite ready, individually or as organizations, for the level of interdependence that would be required to move fast enough to meet the competitive challenges we are all facing. The levels of trust we now need are similar to those that must exist among members of a trapeze troop in a circus. Imagine that, if you can!

The manner in which our little fable has concluded may leave you feeling uneasy. This is intentional. All too often, both you and I have read books or listened to speakers where everything turns out in the end. That is just not realistic; getting comfortable with the discomfort and disappointment of reality is a big part of successfully adopting a CMS practice. Things don't always turn out, and when they don't…where do you turn? In many cases, our experience tells us that when the result is not produced, it is every man or woman for themselves for a while, and productivity takes a hit. Why is it this way? There are lots of reasons; knowing them does not change the fact that in business, as in life, bad news is never welcome.

One of the blessings of the CMS approach—and I have seen this in practice—is that the CMS group itself becomes a foundation to absorb failures and celebrate wins. Bad news, good news…it all becomes the same. News and information is used by the community to formulate the next action steps. Take a look at this diagram, an evolution of the one that Bev introduced in our fable:

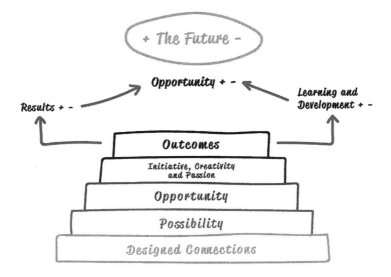

## Theory of A Self Managed Workplace

+ The Future -

Results + -   →   Opportunity + -   ←   Learning and Development + -

Outcomes

Initiative, Creativity and Passion

Opportunity

Possibility

Designed Connections

As you can see, there are some important changes to the diagram. Rather than simply showing INHERITED CONNECTIONS as the foundation layer, you now see DESIGNED CONNECTIONS. It is the continual participation in the CMS that allows members to see where the Connections they have simply assumed with their colleagues and counterparts are insufficient for what they intend to get done. Dialogue needs to take place to allow various members to Design their Connections—dialogues often not available until the members trust and know each other better.

A further evolution occurs when the members distinguish Performance from the mass of Action that takes place in an organization. In the process, they must sort the Action which produces Results from the Action which does not (Activity). This distinction emerges from the morass of explanation that pervades many organizational conversations, as members continue to realize that accountability (doing what you said you would do) creates an environment of integrity where it is possible to see clearly why some Actions produced outcomes and others did not. What this does over time is allow the members to distinguish proposed Actions as Activity based on prior experience or insufficient preparation.

As the members become more strongly connected and better at holding each other to account, they also begin to appreciate that all Results can actually be categorized as Accomplishments. Learning occurs in either case, which can be captured and valued. The combination in any instance of Results and

Learning leaves the group with a New Future—a new place from which to see what they are looking to achieve and very possibly new courses of action.

All of this in itself is a breakthrough, since frequently organizational life tends to go off the rails in the face of unplanned or unpredicted outcomes and events. Time and energy are wasted as efforts are focused on finding a way to "get comfortable." Learning is overlooked or heavily discounted, and whatever new Future perspective might be available is not even recognized. Getting comfortable becomes the objective and usually involves manufacturing an explanation—maybe based in fact, maybe not—that can satisfy the equation WH + GS = O, or Working Hard plus a Good Story becomes the equivalent of the Outcome we were looking for. Once a Good Story is established and accepted, Action can then resume, but almost always while incurring unmeasured psychological and financial costs.

As the CMS matures, members learn that accountability, integrity, and performance are what matters. Comfort, on any occasion, is a bonus and not something to be sought or held in high regard. The resulting condition in a fully matured CMS is a Self-Managing Workplace, where engagement is high and Performance accelerates.

My experience has taught me that the power of the CMS groups comes from its voluntary nature, ASSOCIATION BY CHOICE. Since members of these groups are operating primarily from a discretionary perspective, I have begun to see just how much energy can be unleashed by tapping the lateral capacity revealed when self-interest can be harnessed in a healthy way. Lateral capacity, referred to in Chapter 3, is the capability/energy that is naturally exposed when self-interest is unloosed in service of recognized interdependence. In other words, in a system where my fate and rewards are determined by factors in a dependent CONNECTION like that imposed by traditional hierarchy, my intuitive pull is to serve the interest of the hierarchy without regard to lateral interdependencies that offer no obvious similar benefits. However, when I realize that satisfying the lateral interdependencies indirectly, but unequivocally, satisfies the demands of the dependent CONNECTION, I am drawn to see that it reaches its objectives. And...before you conclude that the CMS process is anti-traditional hierarchy, slow your roll! What the CMS process can do is offset some of the unintended consequences of the apparent, frequently misinterpreted demand imposed by any hierachy.

The people we report to, like us, use available information to make the best decisions they can. They are very rarely trying to make our lives difficult. When we simply follow along with their decisions, based on their limited perspective, we don't do them or ourselves any favors. Members of a CMS have much better information than they've ever had to either make decisions or advise their higher-ups. In addition, they can call upon other CMS members to support them when their input may surprise, or even upset, their own chain of command.

For many reasons, the CMS approach seems to fly in the face of the way the world is going. With the continued advancements in technology showing no signs of slowing, it seems that there is an expectation that everything is going to speed up...but that is not always the case. Certainly, with technology we have the OPPORTUNITY for speed, but that is not all that is required. Remember, humans using inanimate tools like the Internet can go faster and faster depending on the capacity of both the technology and the user. If you have kids and technology in your home, you know exactly what I mean.

On the other hand, if you have humans involved with other humans, technology alone is not necessarily sufficient to realize the full OPPORTUNITY available.

Remember Bev's little diagram...here's where I give you a long-winded view of the world as I see it...

## Theory of Outcomes in Organizations

| Outcomes |
| Action |
| Opportunity |
| Possibility |
| Inherited Connection |

You can see where OPPORTUNITY sits, right? If there is anything to Bev's model, and I think there is, then technology alone obviously doesn't get us where we want to go. Technology in the context of this model is OPPORTUNITY. This concept is frustrating to some people—but not everyone— involved in our workplaces.

So, here I am going to fall back on my 36 years of organizational coaching and advising. Yes, there are mid-level managers for life. They are where they should be, and they should be celebrated for it. Like Bev, they have been offered the chance to move up, but they love what they are doing, where they are doing it, and who they get to do it with. Sound crazy? To some, no doubt it does, but I invite you to take a leap of faith with me. This is based on my experience…

What I have learned is not everyone who goes into management is interested in rising as far upward as they can. In fact, those inclined to unlimited upward mobility are a very small population. Thank goodness for this because, with the pyramidal shape of most organizations, there is not much room at the top. I, for one, am glad for those people too because they are inclined to want to run things, they have the talent for it, and they are the ones who keep us pressing for those double-digit earnings. They also are best-suited for the politics needed to move into the future when the future is always just somebody's best guess. Big risk usually garners big reward, and that small fraction of people who are energized and drawn to play the power games create continued employment opportunities for the rest of us. It is this small fraction of our workforce—of any workforce—that allows for mid-level managers to pursue the kind of work they enjoy: developing people, with a relatively reduced level of risk, while knowing someone is looking out for the bigger picture.

But there are some drawbacks to counting on this small fraction of what I will call drivers—people like Carolyn, bless her heart. Unfortunately, they, while driving themselves, tend to think that everyone should operate like them. They have limited patience for, or understanding of, the rest of us.

Here's my approximation of reality—at least, the reality I have experienced: 80–85 percent of people in the workplace, managers included, need a solid CONNECTION before they can take full advantage of whatever OPPORTUNITY is available. That doesn't mean they can't get things done with weak connections; they do it all the time. Think about the people you work with. In many instances, you are getting things done daily with co-workers with whom the only real connection you have is that you work for the same employer. In many, if not most, instances, that's good enough. And then there are the other times; the times when you need someone to go that extra distance for you or provide that special favor. You don't go to the weak connections; you would not count on weak connections in these cases. You look for, and hopefully find, someone to whom you have a strong connection, someone who has some amount of commitment to your success—which is what happens when your work affects them and vice versa. It is this principle, the principle of the strong connection, that is the secret of the CMS process.

Allow me to refer back to Bev's diagram for a moment. Just above Association by Choice, you'll see a layer identified as POSSIBILITY. This is often read as PROBABILITY or PREDICTABILITY.

How I would like you to read it is as "way in hell!" This would then infer that the absence of POSSIBILITY might well be labeled "no way in hell!" If you've been alive for a while, there are a couple of things you have come to understand about life: a) there is no free lunch, and b) there are no guarantees.

Okay, you say, so what? Here's what. Let's say you need something in hurry—a pair of pants cleaned and pressed, and it's after the deadline posted by the dry cleaner in the window, and you've never done business with this dry cleaner, and the 18-year-old with the ear buds behind the counter has just locked the door. Chances are good that you know there is "no way in hell" you are getting your pants done there. Starting to get it?

So, as you look again through the window you think you recognize the teenager as one of your son's friends from school; you seem to recall he has even been over to the house. Suddenly you see "way in hell" if you can get the kid to acknowledge the connection. You pound on the window, softly of course; he looks up, and you can see from the smile on his face that you may be saved. No guarantee, of course, just like the rest of life, but I bet you get the difference. It is a visceral experience, and you know when it's there and when it's not.

Life is so much different when you know you have at least a shot at success.

The reason a CMS works is that members have a stake in each other's success. Now, unlike the kid in the dry-cleaning example, the stake works both ways; your success depends on mine, and mine depends on yours. This relationship is one of the drawbacks of the functional organization. Generally, the hierarchy is organized by function, and interdependencies are obscured or at least mitigated by the reward structure. It seems pretty obvious that whatever impacts our compensation impacts our actions as well. If the reward structure does not take into account the interdependencies, then the chances of us realizing ASSOCIATION BY CHOICE where we most need it are based on personal connection unsupported by organizational structure. Put plainly, I hope the teenager does not have a commitment to meet his girlfriend when I ask him to open up and stay late for my pants. I don't want to compete with that hierarchical concern!

So, back to going slow and getting started. Here's kind of the rule: Whatever you don't cover at the beginning of any attempt to produce an organizational result will get you in the end if it was indeed necessary. Time and time again, we've all set out to get something accomplished and not taken enough time on the front end to cover the necessary foundational concerns, only to find out in the middle of the project that there is no way to produce the result without covering the foundational concerns. In the middle of the process it gets very expensive. If you've got any managerial experience, you know exactly what I am talking about!

Finally, how do you get a CMS up and running? It takes time because, unlike ordinary problem solving, you are using the necessity of producing a result as an excuse to build capacity into your organization. It is this capacity that was previously missing and gave you the problem you are setting out to correct. Once the capacity is built, you not only don't have the problem anymore, you have both new POSSIBILITY AND OPPORTUNITY. In other words, you can take on challenges you could not previously imagine. I am not going to say trust me because that would make you crazy, and I don't want that. But, I will say try it.

Remember, a CMS is not a formula; it is a framework for development and PERFORMANCE. As such, the steps that follow are not necessarily linear; some can take place simultaneously and will, simply because we are working with people and with people it is always messy. When I teach my MBA students about managing people, I always start with a caveat: "With people, you never know what's going to work until it does." So, long story short, follow these steps…but just keep plugging.

—

Step 1) Choose your initial CMS group based on your knowledge of the managers who are most likely to see the OPPORTUNITY in what you are talking about. These are the managers who are consistently involved in cross-functional communication, don't shrink from confronting cross-functional breakdowns, and understand that mistakes happen but everything can be worked out in conversation.

Step 2) Once you are in communication with the people you think have the highest chance of success, ask them to do two things. First, identify the lingering issue they want to tackle and identify the payback for effort. Second, identify the cross-functional counterparts they believe they need to work with to achieve their objective.

Step 3) Go to your counterparts in the areas that will need to be involved, and take the time to engage their support. Knowing full well that there might be skepticism, ask for a six-month commitment before any judgment is passed. It helps to make sure the payback you identify is sufficiently significant to overcome any skepticism, at least for six months. It will help if your counterparts can see their own self-interest being improved if your theories become reality.

Step 4) Enlist the support and partnership of people in your Talent group, if you have one. With their help, identify someone you think would be an appropriate facilitator for the newly formed CMS. This is not time to use rookies or enthusiasts. This is work for experienced management developers who have some connection, if possible, to the group they will be serving.

Step 5) Launch, but softly. No hats, tee shirts, mugs, or banners. A CMS is not a process or a program; it is a **practice**...here's the way we defined practice at our launch...*repeated exercise in or performance of an activity or skill so as to acquire or maintain proficiency in it.* You don't want to scare anybody off, so ask initially for a six-month commitment, and get it from everyone before you accept their participation in the CMS.

Step 6) Outline the CMS Session format. Three hours once a month on regularly scheduled dates and times, voluntary participation but mandatory attendance at all sessions. (See Guidelines in Chapter 16.) Half of each session should be devoted to ongoing reflective engagement with some conceptual area of the practice of managing, such as handling tough conversations, establishing a foundation for coaching, or identifying candidates for upward development. (See CoachingOurselves.com) The purpose of this approach is to have the managers in the CMS group recognize that they already know more than they realize about managing from their direct experience. They may just lack a shared vocabulary that allows them to discuss and deliberate management issues effectively with their colleagues. The second half of each session will be devoted initially to identifying and processing (problem solving) issues directly related to the measurable improvement they have gathered to achieve. Each session begins with a review of commitments made in the previous session, and ends with commitments to take action before the next session.

Now, if this design sounds too simplistic, I understand. Here's what I ask you to do: Make a commitment to follow the process steps I just outlined for six months. Once you've got your CMS members assembled and a facilitator on board, make sure they make the same commitment. Then, just get going. Do not expect miracles at the start—in fact, don't expect anything—just follow the process and pay attention, measure what you set out to improve, and notice when people don't do what they say they will. In the end, my bet is the learning that will ensue will be as valuable as the results you produce, and the bond that will form among members will buy you another six months of working together.

What I have come to see is that there is no beginning, middle, and end for a CMS group. There is a beginning and, as long as the interdependencies remain intact, the value of the process will continue to be realized. That is what makes this practice revolutionary.

Early in my career, I had a manager who advised me to not be too concerned about failures on individual projects. He said, "Mike, this is a lot like sports, only the seasons in business are only separated by a day, December 31 ends one season, and January 1 starts another. In many sports, 100 percent isn't the goal; it's the overall performance that matters. We must determine what game we are playing, and what winning looks like in that game. Some games are harder than others. In fact, some games, like hitting a baseball, are so hard that being successful 30 percent of the time will get you paid several million dollars a year and winning two thirds of your games will get you a championship. Imagine that!"

Based on his counsel, I've decided that each CMS is its own sport with its own measures of success. A CMS should not be judged against any others; each is unique and should be judged against itself by its own members. A measure of CMS success where results are consolidated would produce a nonsensical picture of CMS value and effectiveness.

How long should a CMS last? As long as the members see value in gathering each month, and as long as they can demonstrate value to the organization, I see no reason why any individual CMS would not continue indefinitely. Remember, it is a practice, not a process. When are you so physically fit that you can say you don't need to exercise anymore?

Lastly, remember this: Once upon a time, man could not fly. After many attempts and many failures, we are now able to move about our planet with unprecedented degrees of freedom. It was trial and error that got us where we are today; not smooth, unfailing project plans. Those to whom we give initial credit could likely not have accomplished what they did without the failures of those who went before them. I imagine all those would-be flyers would understand the following quote...

> "If I don't manage to fly someone else will.
> The Spirit wants only that there be flying.
> And for who happens to do it,
> In that he has only a passing interest."
>
> —Rainer Maria Rilke

Establishing a CMS is not about who gets credit; it is about replacing that worn-out admonition, "We have to learn to work smarter not harder!" with a new aspiration: "When you reach the end of your road, it is time to learn to fly!"

# APPENDIX A

## USING ENLIGHTENED SELF-INTEREST TO STAY SANE, PRODUCTIVE, AND AMUSED AT WORK

### 15 Guidelines for Staying Engaged at all Times, with Questions for Reflection

Here are some guidelines developed by other CMS groups for staying clear-headed and centered as you participate with your CMS.

### 1.) Show up.

This should be self-evident but is often overlooked. The likelihood of you contributing is dependent on your full engagement.

- Where are you currently involved but going through the motions?

- What are you committed to that you have let others influence without making your thoughts known?

### 2.) Whoever sees it first gets to do it.

This is the principle of *Responsibility*. There is no validity to the statement "That's not my responsibility" until you say so.

- What needs to be done right now in your immediate environment that you've been waiting for someone else to pick up the ball on?

- Recall and describe an instance where you saw what needed to be done, didn't wait for permission or ask whether you ought to be doing it, and just did the right thing.

### 3.) Nobody likes anybody's ideas better than their own.

This is the principle of *Participation*. Everyone wants to play, and they will play your game if they can play their way; let them.

- What are you trying to get done right now that requires the help of others, but you are attached to having it done your way?

- Recall and describe a time when your enthusiasm was squashed by someone insisting that a task or project be done in a way you were not in favor of.

**4.) Ordinary life will provide as much nonsense as you can deal with; do not contribute to the confusion.**

This is the principle of *Persistence*. There is normally nothing and no one assigned to your success. At the same time, there is nothing and no one assigned to make sure you do not succeed. Whining is not a good substitute for performance, and it adds to the mess.

- What are you pouting about right now?

- Recall and describe an instance where the nonsense just became more than you were willing to deal with.

**5.) Do not confuse your beliefs with the truth; it makes you stupid and an annoyance to other people.**

This is the principle of *Perspective*. Your "point of view" is valid, as "your point of view." As "the point," it makes life around you really crummy for everyone concerned. Behave yourself!

- Where are you currently being constrained by one of your beliefs?

- Recall and describe a situation where someone put their relationship with you at risk over a belief they held dear.

**6.) When you have no control, you must communicate. When you do not communicate, apologize. When someone fails to communicate with you, forgive.**

This is the principle of *Traveling Light*. Life is challenging enough all by itself; don't collect or create baggage.

- Where do you have something to say to someone that has gone on far too long?

- Recall and describe a time someone finally told you they had been upset with you for a long time.

**7.) Manage mutual understanding.**

This is the principle of *Relationship*. Never leave your motive or your intent up to someone's imagination. If you do, chances are good they'll think the worst. Communication is a process inside a relationship inside a context, not a transaction.

- When have you received a communication that you badly misinterpreted?

- Recall and describe a time when someone misread your intentions and assumed bad motive on your part.

**8.) Give up your right to say, "I told you so!"**

This is the principle of *Partnership*. If you don't say it or you've had your say, forget it, shut up, and get to work.

- When have you reminded someone, after the fact, that they should have listened to you?

- Recall and describe a time when someone let you know that if you had listened to them they could have saved you from making a mistake.

**9.) We are all, as individuals, in over our heads. That's just the way it is.**

The greatest barrier we all face to living a productive and satisfying life is our willingness to ask for help. This is the principle of *Interdependence,* the foundational principle of all life and existence.

- Are you treading water right now, telling yourself it is no big deal, when you should be asking for help?

- Recall and describe a time when you saw someone fail when they could have asked for help?

**10.) Keep your expectations consistent with only what has been promised. Anything else you get is a bonus, and you have no basis for ever expecting to get it again.**

This is the principle of *Living as Though Nothing is Guaranteed.* Everyone, you included, is dealing with multiple commitments and multiple audiences. Do yourself a favor, recognize how your limitations conflict with your own intent to meet everyone's needs, and notice how often you say "yes" just so you can get back to what you think is most important.

Also, notice that, no matter how hard you work, someone always ends up disappointed and you end up apologizing.

- When have you been disappointed because you hoped for something that had not really been promised?

- Recall and describe a time when you should have said no and ended up disappointing someone.

**11.) Limit your opinions to only those things which you are truly committed and prepared to act upon.**

This is so hard; we really live like we have a right to our opinions about everything. It is hard enough to keep our emotions in check and remain productive and clear-headed without constantly stoking the fires of upset by tossing opinion after opinion onto the pile.

- What do you currently have a strong opinion about that really doesn't matter much to you?

- Recall and describe a time when someone got upset with you about something you hadn't known mattered to them.

**12.) Toughen up.**

Life is a contact sport anyway; organizational life is worse! It is not personal, and you will get injured no matter how hard you try to be invisible. Be prepared to heal quickly and throw an elbow yourself occasionally.

- When were you wounded in a way that took a long time to get over? Maybe you are not over it yet!

- Recall and describe a time when you took a licking and kept on ticking.

**13.) Get curious—stay curious.**

This is the principle of *Humility*. Some of us are born with a natural curiosity about the world around us. Consider yourself blessed. Most of us are not so fortunate; we may be smart, but we learn as required. Staying engaged is a function of getting out in front of the known and asking what unknown would be worth knowing.

- Where can you admit that it is time for you to learn something new?

- Recall a time that what you learned came as a complete surprise.

**14.) Give your gifts willingly.**

This is the principle of *Generosity.* What seems mundane to you may be miraculous for me if I have not been blessed with the same talents you have. Share what you have been given so that you may receive what you do not have. This may seem obvious, but nothing could be sadder than to die with gifts unused.

- Where are you holding back? You have something to offer, and it is time to get involved!

- Recall a time when someone's generosity changed your life.

**15.) Remember...if you can't laugh at yourself, someone else will always be happy to do it for you.**

Embrace the interdependence; it is the path to both success and satisfaction.

- What is the most embarrassing thing you have ever experienced?

- Recall and describe a time when you laughed very hard at yourself over a mistake you made.

# APPENDIX B

## THE DISTRIBUTED DEVELOPMENT
## COMMUNITY

The Communities of Mutual Success (CMS) described in *Thriving in the Middle* are a form of Distributed Development Community (DDC). This approach to development was originally pioneered by the open-source software community. Historically associated with projects with clearly defined objectives, the CMS as portrayed here is an adaptation of a highly collaborative process with a specified outcome for an ongoing purpose; that is, the professional development of the community members themselves using measurable outputs as evidence of progress and value.

As contrasted to the traditional DDC, where there is a defined objective and a project with beginning, middle, and end, the CMS has a beginning and progressive maturation that produces an increased performance capacity—the net of contribution of the assembled members. The CMS will have a life span determined primarily by the value it produces for members, as well as the performance it produces for the organization in which it resides.

A CMS is ideally 6–12 members. Multiples of three are recommended, simply for the ease of smaller group interactions. Materials, such as those produced by CoachingOurselves, are ideal for the practice of a CMS in that they contain the content and questions to guide peer-coaching around specific themes and soft skills. Managers and leaders, with or without the support of an external facilitator coach, can use a series of CoachingOurselves modules aligned with organizational needs. This enables the delivery of broad-based impacts as the organization builds the capacity to develop itself.

This approach does not spell the end of classroom development. Rather, the CMS becomes the focal point of development, and the classroom, while remaining necessary, becomes supplemental to the ongoing practice of development.

# ENDNOTES

[1]Hedges, K. (2014, Sept. 23). "If You Think Leadership Development is a Waste of Time, You May Be Right." Forbes. Retrieved from http://www.forbes.com/sites/work-in-progress/2014/09/23/if-you-think-leadership-development-is-a-waste-of-time-you-may-be-right/-448298d25dcc2f542cdc5dcc

[2] Kegan, R. & Lahey, L.L. (2009). Immunity to Change: How to Overcome it and Unlock the Potential in Yourself and Your Organization (Leadership for the Common Good). Boston, Massachusetts: Harvard Business School Publishing.

[3]Kegan, R. & Lahey, L.L. (2009). Immunity to Change: How to Overcome it and Unlock the Potential in Yourself and Your Organization (Leadership for the Common Good). Boston, Massachusetts: Harvard Business School Publishing.

[4] Adapted from Ronald A. Heifetz & Donald L. Laurie, "The Work of Leadership," Harvard Business Review, January-February 1997; and Ronald A. Heifetz & Marty Linsky, Leadership on the Line, Harvard Business School Press, 2002

[5] Ibid.

[6] Morgan McCall and colleagues at The Center for Creative Leadership are usually credited with originating the 70-20-10 ratio.

# MIKE COOK

CEO MENTOR, COACHING,
MANAGEMENT DEVELOPMENT

A former Human Resource professional for Standard Oil of California, Mike now works primarily with senior leaders and teams to develop and implement communities of collaborative performance. He enjoys working with diverse client teams at all levels to build alignment and enable change that is sustainable and strategic. Mike has 30+ years consulting/coaching experience working in a wide range of industries and working environments as a designer, facilitator, coach, and project team lead on major cultural change initiatives. His experience includes initiatives in petroleum refining, telecommunications, financial services, healthcare, and insurance systems.

Since his move to the San Juan Islands in 2006 Mike has founded AMJ Group, a solo practice focused on developing peer level manager's collaborative work communities. Prior to arriving in Anacortes, WA, Mike founded Vitalwork, Inc. a diverse Organizational Development firm, in Rochester, NY. From 1989 to early 2011 Mike served Vitalwork as CEO and Senior Consultant. He has directly overseen several projects at both Eastman Kodak and Xerox Corporations that directly impacted those businesses' ability to deliver new products to market in a timelier, higher quality manner. He also designed and led the implementation process for Frontier Communications as it moved its employee base from a regulated telecom to an open market business operating model.

Since 2012 Mike has served as a member of the Adjunct Faculty for Western Washington University's MBA program focusing on Managing Organizations and People.

More recently (2016) Mike has affiliated with Vistage Worldwide. He currently serves as an advisor and council to CEO's and Executives of mid-size businesses in the Northwest Washington area.

A prolific writer, Mike has authored the book *THRIVE: Standing on Your Own Two Feet in a Borderless World* in 2006 and has published numerous articles in popular publications. He currently writes a bi-weekly column for the Bellingham Business Journal focused on issues related to middle management.

70830314R00101

Made in the USA
Lexington, KY
15 November 2017